A CHARLIE BROWN CHRISTMAS

A CHARLIE BROWN CHRISTMAS

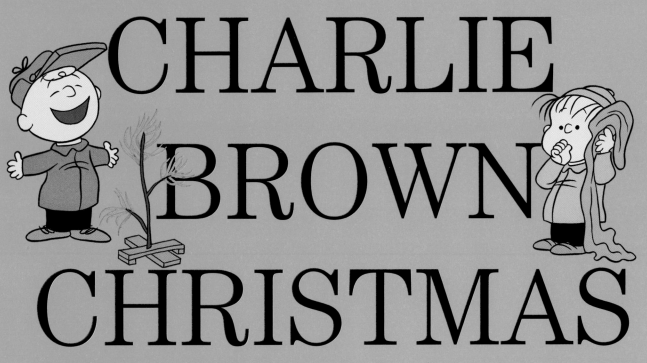

THE MAKING OF A TRADITION

by Lee Mendelson with Reflections by Bill Melendez

Edited by Antonia Felix   Designed by Timothy Shaner

Schulz

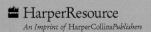
HarperResource
An Imprint of HarperCollinsPublishers

For Sparky . . . we'll never forget you.

Photograph/art credits and permissions: Mendelson-Melendez Productions: front matter, 6–79, 86. David Guaraldi: 15, 80–85, 87–92. Complete Post, Inc., Hollywood, California: cover, stills from the animated film on pages 100–192 and flip art on pages 7–191. Advertisements on pages 30 and 32 courtesy of the Academy of Motion Pictures Arts and Sciences. "Peanuts on Television" reprinted with permission from TV Guide ©1965 TV Guide Magazine Group, Inc. TV Guide is a registered trademark of TV Guide Magazine Group, Inc. Time cover on page 14 reprinted with permission from TIME/TIMEPIX. "Christmas Time is Here" and "Linus and Lucy" © 1997 CPP Belwin, a division of Warner Bros.

A CHARLIE BROWN CHRISTMAS: THE MAKING OF A TRADITION

HarperCollins books may be purchased for educational, business, or sales promotional use. For information, please write to: Special Markets Department, HarperCollins Publishers Inc., 10 East 53rd Street, New York, New York 10022.

FIRST EDITION

Library of Congress Cataloging-in-Publication Data

Schulz, Charles M.
    A Charlie Brown Christmas: the making of a tradition /Charles Schulz.
        p. cm.
    ISBN 0-06-019851-6
    1. Charlie Brown Christmas (Television program) I. Title.

PN1992.77.C45 S38 2000
791.45'72—dc21   00-044889

00 01 02 03 04 QWC 10 0 9 7 6 5 4 3 2 1

http://www.harpercollins.com
Printed in Canada

contents

preface

by lee mendelson
executive producer

on saturday afternoon, February 12, 2000, I was talking on the phone with Charles Schulz. It was not unlike thousands of phone calls that we had shared over thirty-seven years on various projects.

He had been thrilled the night before by a tribute we had produced with CBS News, hosted by one of his heroes, Walter Cronkite. It was just one of hundreds of tributes he had received from around the world since his retirement.

We talked about the preparation for this book. *A Charlie Brown Christmas* had always been his favorite of the forty-five specials we had produced with animator Bill Melendez. He was excited about our retelling of how it all came about. We also talked about the story line for our next animated show, *Marbles,* which he had just sent off to Bill to be storyboarded.

Charles Schulz's final comic strip was to appear the next day. It would be number 18,170 in over forty-nine years of drawing nonstop. He told me that as he was writing this last strip he had looked up and said aloud, almost in disbelief, "I just realized . . . that poor little guy is never going to kick that football. Good grief!"

LEFT: Lee Mendelson meeting with Charles Schulz, foreground, for the first time, in 1963. They discussed creating a documentary about Sparky's life and work.

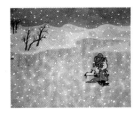

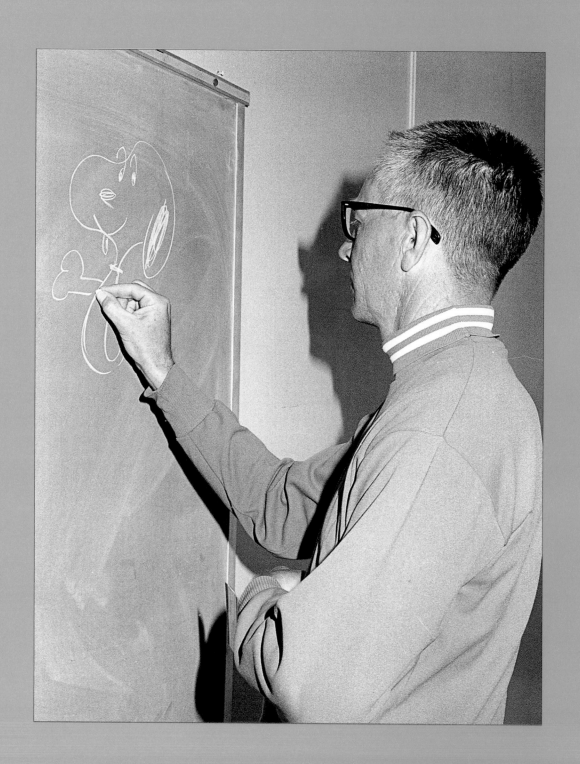

At that moment I realized—more than ever—how real Charlie Brown and his gang had been for their creator.

We planned to meet the next day at his home. A few hours later, my friend of nearly four decades passed away in his sleep.

I was not surprised by the worldwide reaction to his passing. He was at once an artist, a philosopher, a humorist, and most of all, a true gentleman. A shy man who ironically was the first cartoonist to bring emotions and feelings to the comics!

There was a single night in December of 1969 when a *Peanuts* movie was playing to a sold-out audience at the Radio City Music Hall, *You're a Good Man, Charlie Brown* was playing to a sold-out audience Off-Broadway, and *A Charlie Brown Christmas* was being watched by half of the American television audience—after a hundred million of us had read his comic strip earlier that day! All because of one man, one genius, one brilliant cartoonist who loved his country passionately.

His friends all called him Sparky, and he never lost the common touch. This is the story of how he created a television milestone.

Lee Mendelson

LEFT: Charles Schulz chalks one up in this candid photograph from 1968.

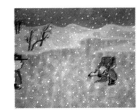

HOLLY

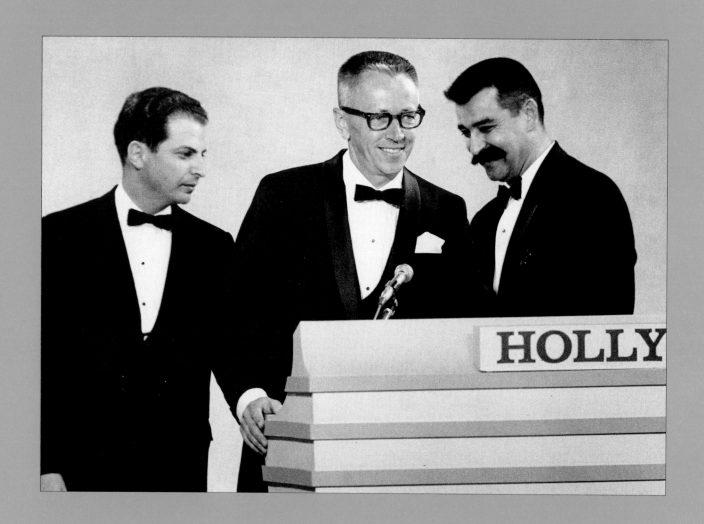

the making of a tradition

by lee mendelson

ironically, there's a connection between the world's greatest baseball player and the world's worst baseball player—and it leads to the production of *A Charlie Brown Christmas.*

In 1963, soon after I had formed my independent production company just south of San Francisco, I produced a documentary on Willie Mays that was broadcast on the NBC-TV network.

A few weeks later, I was reading a *Peanuts* comic strip in which Charlie Brown was losing another baseball game. The idea of following my first special about the world's "greatest" with a program about the world's "worst" just popped into my mind. By 1963, thirteen years after its debut in a handful of newspapers, *Peanuts,* featuring "Good Ol' Charlie Brown," had already become the most famous comic strip in the world. The book *Happiness Is a Warm Puppy* was #1 on the national bestseller lists. Fans were taking home *Peanuts* calendars, plush Snoopy dolls, and other enormously successful merchandise.

I called Charles Schulz at his home in Sebastopol, California. Fortunately, being an avid baseball fan, Sparky had seen and enjoyed *A Man Named Mays*. I told him that I would like to produce a documentary about his life and about the world of "Good Ol' Charlie Brown." He invited me to come out and visit him so that we could discuss the project.

Sparky and I had a very cordial meeting and we decided to produce a half-hour docu-

LEFT: Charles Schulz accepts the Emmy for Best Network Animated Special in 1966 for *A Charlie Brown Christmas,* flanked by executive producer Lee Mendelson, left, and director/animator Bill Melendez, right.

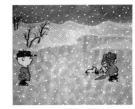

mentary. I wanted to include one or two minutes of animation (which was all I could afford at the time), and Sparky told me to get in touch with animator Bill Melendez. Sparky and Bill had collaborated on the first-ever animation of *Peanuts* a few years back for the Ford Motor Company. Bill, who was then working for a company called Playhouse Pictures, had started out with The Walt Disney Company in the late 1930s and early 1940s, working on such animated classics as *Pinocchio, Fantasia, Dumbo,* and *Bambi.*

While Bill was creating two minutes of animation based on a few comic strips, Sparky and I started to shoot the documentary. We filmed him in his studio, drawing and discussing the characters. We also filmed him in his daily routine, capturing everything from driving his five children to school to bowling at night. As we filmed in the bowling alley, one of the local residents came over and said to me, "I don't know what you're filming this for, but we have much better bowlers over there on my lane." Later that night at a gas station, the attendant came over and asked Sparky if Charlie Brown was ever going to kick the football. Sparky replied, "Probably not." For the next thirty-seven years that proved to be true.

Once we completed filming I had to add some music. I had always been a great fan of jazz, and while driving back from Sparky's over the Golden Gate Bridge I heard a song called "Cast Your Fate to the Wind." The radio announcer said it had won a Grammy and had been written and performed by a San Franciscan named Vince Guaraldi. I called Ralph Gleason, jazz critic of the *San Francisco Chronicle*, and he put me in touch with Vince. It turned out that Vince was a great fan of *Peanuts* and he agreed to work on the music.

12

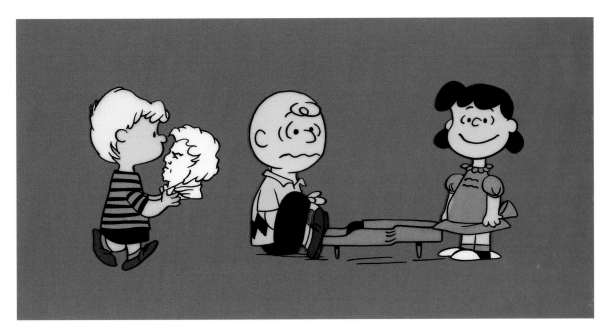

ABOVE: A scene from the animation included in *A Boy Named Charlie Brown*. Although the documentary was never sold to a network, the two minutes of animation by Bill Melendez caught the eye of Coca-Cola. They asked Lee Mendelson if he could produce an animated Christmas special, and *A Charlie Brown Christmas* was born.

RIGHT: In the final scene of *A Boy Named Charlie Brown*, Lee Mendelson introduces Sparky, who is being honored by the San Francisco Giants at Candlestick Park.

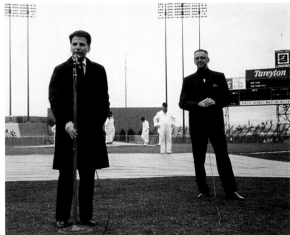

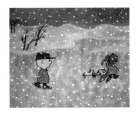

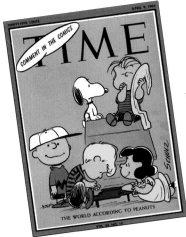

A few weeks later Vince called me, very excited. He said he wanted to play something he had just written. I told him that I would prefer to come hear it at his studio rather than over the telephone, but he said he couldn't wait. "I've got to play this for someone right now or I'll *explode!*" he said. I told him to go ahead, and what I heard over the next two minutes stunned me. It was perfect for the *Peanuts* characters! When he returned to the phone, I asked him what he was going to call it. He said, "Linus and Lucy." Little did we know that years later this piece would become a jazz standard throughout the world.

We finished the documentary and as a test I showed it to the San Francisco Advertising Club. Everyone raved about the show and I was confident that it would be an easy sell to either a network or a sponsor. But in true Charlie Brown fashion, no one was interested. (Seven years later, only slightly modified, the documentary won an Emmy.)

For over a year and a half, after meetings with all the networks and all the major sponsors, I had just about given up on selling the Charles Schulz film. Then, in April of 1965, *Time* magazine did a story about Sparky and the *Peanuts* gang and featured all the characters on the cover. A few weeks later I received a call from John Allen at the McCann Erickson Agency in New York. He had seen and liked our documentary, and for a moment I thought he had called to possibly buy it for one of his clients. John had already been responsible for launching the *National Geographic* documentaries, so I was very excited. But he had a different message for me: "Have you and Mr. Schulz ever considered doing a Christmas special?" he asked.

ABOVE: *Time* magazine ran a *Peanuts* cover story in April 1965, when Lee Mendelson was still trying to sell his documentary about Charles Schulz to a network. This major piece of national publicity was one more factor that led to Coca-Cola's interest in sponsoring a Christmas special—an animated show starring the *Peanuts* characters.

14

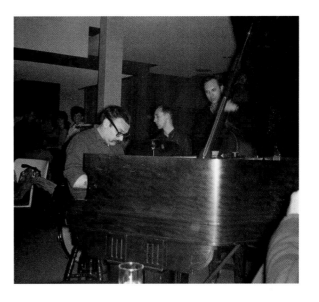

"Of course," I replied, not bothering to think about what I was saying.

"Well," John continued, "the good news is that one of my clients, Coca-Cola, is looking for a Christmas special. The bad news is that today is Wednesday and they'll need an outline in Atlanta by Monday. Do you think that's possible?"

"Of course," I replied, again not bothering to think before I spoke.

John said, "Okay. They'd like it to be a half-hour show. Good luck."

I hung up the phone and stared at it for a few minutes. Then I called Sparky. "I think I may have just sold a Charlie Brown Christmas show," I said. "And what show might that be?" Sparky asked. "The one you need to make an outline for tomorrow," I replied. Without missing a beat, he calmly said, "Okay. Come on up."

The next day I took notes as Sparky outlined his ideas. "If it's to be a Christmas special, I want to certainly deal with the true

RIGHT: Jazz pianist/composer Vince Guaraldi playing at a club in his hometown, San Francisco. Lee Mendelson hired Guaraldi to write music for his Schulz documentary after hearing the pianist's Grammy-winning "Cast Your Fate to the Wind" on the radio.

"The good news is that one of my clients, Coca-Cola, is looking for a Christmas special. The bad news is that today is Wednesday and they'll need an outline in Atlanta by Monday. Do you think that's possible?"

—*John Allen to Lee Mendelson*

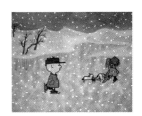

Far down in the forest, where the warm sun and the fresh air made a sweet resting-place, grew a pretty little fir tree.

"Oh! how I wish I were as tall as the other trees, then I would spread out my branches on every side, and my top would over-look the wide world. I should have the birds building their nests on my boughs, and when the wind blew, I should bow with stately dignity like my tall companions.

"Oh, if I could but keep on growing tall and old! There is nothing else worth caring for in the world!"

—From "The Fir Tree" by Hans Christian
Andersen, translated by H. P. Paull

Lee Mendelson and his wife had read this
Christmas story to their children during the
holiday season of 1964, a few months before
the making of *A Charlie Brown Christmas*.
Lee's memory of it inspired him to suggest
using a tree in the story line of the show.
Charles Schulz seized on the idea and came
up with a tree only Charlie Brown could love.

meaning of Christmas," he said. "And I'd like to do a lot of scenes in the snow and with skating." (He grew up in St. Paul, Minnesota, after all!) "And maybe we can do something with a Christmas play and mix some of that jazz music with traditional music." His ideas flowed nonstop, and by the end of the day I sent a complete outline to Coca-Cola in Atlanta (an outline that, basically, would never change as the show evolved).

Days went by and we heard nothing. John Allen was in Europe and we had no other contact with his agency. Although I felt sure that we had a winner, doubts started to creep in when there was no response. Then, after three weeks had passed, John called me. I stopped breathing when he started to speak. "Well, once again I have good news and bad news," he said. "The good news is that Coca-Cola wants to buy *A Charlie Brown Christmas,* but the bad news is they want it for early December. That gives you just six months. Can you do it in six months?"

I could barely get the words out as I blurted, "Of course!"—again without having any idea if it was possible. "Good," John said. "You'll hear from our business affairs people tomorrow. Get to work. And," he concluded, "congratulations."

"The core of the program had already been established in the outline which had gone to our sponsor: the show would include winter scenes, a school play, a scene to be read from the Bible, and a sound track combining jazz and traditional music."

—Lee Mendelson

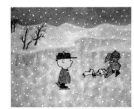

17

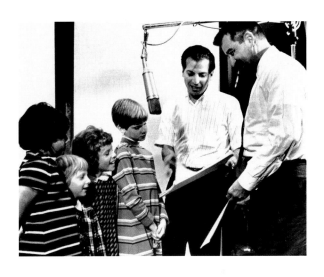

After a few moments of total exhilaration followed by a few seconds of utter panic, I quickly called Bill Melendez, who by 1965 had formed his own animation company. "Can we do an animated half hour in six months?" I asked. "Of course!" he immediately replied, and I wondered if his "Of course" had any more substance than mine. But he sounded very confident and we agreed to meet with Sparky within the next few days.

Bill, Sparky, and I all met in Sparky's studio. The core of the program had already been established in the outline that had gone to our sponsor: the show would include winter scenes, a school play, a scene to be read from the Bible, and a sound track combining jazz and traditional music. On the previous Christmas, my wife and I had read Hans

LEFT AND RIGHT: Unlike the usual Hollywood practice of hiring adult actors to mimic the voices of children, *A Charlie Brown Christmas* featured the voices of real children—a choice that gave the show a refreshing innocence. Director/animator Bill Melendez works with four young cast members in the recording studio. From left to right are Gai DeFaria; Lynda Mendelson (Lee's daughter); Anne Altieri, who played Frieda in *A Charlie Brown Christmas;* and Sally Dryer, who played Violet. In this session the cast is recording *It Was a Short Summer, Charlie Brown*, which aired in 1969.

"We realized that Charlie Brown's voice had to be 'blah'; Lucy's had to be assertive and even crabby; Linus's would have to combine intelligence with childlike simplicity, as he was someone who cherished his thumb and blanket."

—Lee Mendelson

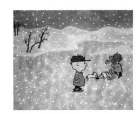

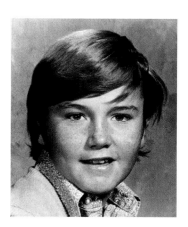

Christian Andersen's "The Fir Tree" to our kids and I thought that we might do something involving a tree. Sparky immediately seized on that idea and said, "We need a Charlie Brown-like tree." But my next suggestion did not get the same response. "A lot of the animated shows have laugh tracks, and maybe . . . ."

"Absolutely not," said Sparky.

And that was that.

We talked about having a theme song to open the show—music that was neither traditional nor jazz. We also wanted to create a scene that could feature the Vince Guaraldi "Linus and Lucy" theme from the 1963 Schulz documentary—a scene that eventually became the dance segment that viewers remember so vividly. Sparky also wanted a scene with Schroeder playing Beethoven, so we had quite a musical mixture in the offing.

In the comic strips, Snoopy always had the best gags and the best jokes, so we had to have those in the show as well. But we couldn't have him actually talk; we had to rely on animation to make him do things that he couldn't do in the strip. In the process, we gained a veritable "canine Harpo Marx."

Then we discussed the other voices. We realized that Charlie Brown's voice had to be "blah"; Lucy's had to be assertive and even crabby; Linus's would have to combine intelligence with childlike simplicity, as he was someone who cherished his thumb and blanket. Bill suggested that for Snoopy's "sounds" he would just talk gibberish and then speed up the tape. Bill thus became the "voice" of Snoopy (and later on, Woodstock) for thirty-seven years.

Sparky wrote the script and Bill put it on a storyboard. A storyboard page contains six squares (six scenes per page). There are about eighty pages to a storyboard, so Bill would create 480 scenes with the dialogue from the script appearing under each scene.

Next, we auditioned dozens and dozens of kids for the key roles. Charlie Brown, who had to sound bland but also had to be a good actor, required an unusual combination of talent. We found the perfect voice and performer in eight-and-a-half-year-old Peter Robbins, and he became our first Charlie Brown. Already an old hat at show biz, Peter

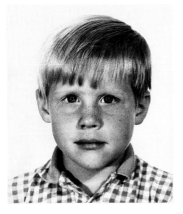

had appeared in the movie *A Ticklish Affair,* several television series including "F Troop" and "Get Smart," and more than thirty-five television commercials. Peter, who is now in his forties, spoke to me about his memories of recording in the studio.

"I thought it was going to be very easy; a voice-over compared to acting on camera," said Peter. "But once I got in the studio I found it was chaotic, with a bunch of kids, six to nine years old, running all over the place and too excited to calm down. We had unusual words to deliver like 'good grief' and 'rats' and 'eastern syndicate.' A lot of the talk was 'edgy,' at least for us kids at the time. Another challenge was the fact that I, as Charlie Brown, was supposed to be depressed at Christmastime. It was very strange for an eight-and-a-half-year-old to pretend to be depressed about Christmas, the most joyous time of the year!"

Peter pulled it off, of course, and somehow all the kids settled down and got to work. "We did the whole show in a few hours," said Peter. "I'll never forget that day."

Peter's remarks echo the thoughts that had been expressed by many of our potential clients over the years. One of the reasons we couldn't sell an animated *Peanuts* show for such a long time was the fact that the clients felt that the kids in the comic strip often expressed adult thoughts and used adult words. As Peter recalled, even the child actors themselves were somewhat mystified by the dialogue.

Peter Robbins went on to play Charlie Brown in the next five specials as well as the first *Peanuts* movie. His godmother was the famous Hollywood agent Hazel McMillen. She found us our first Linus, another child actor who had gone out on many auditions with Peter. Hazel called me and said, "I have this wonderful actor but he has a very slight lisp. He can read with great emotion, however." She sent us Christopher Shea, and as soon as he read his first passage we knew we had our

ABOVE LEFT: Eight-and-a-half-year-old Peter Robbins, the voice of Charlie Brown in *A Charlie Brown Christmas*. ABOVE: Seven-year-old Christopher Shea, the voice of Linus in the show.

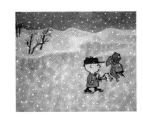

Linus. His slight lisp gave him a youthful sweetness while his emotional delivery gave him power and authority as well.

Seven-year-old Christopher Shea had been acting since age four, and in his child acting career he played Linus in our first five *Peanuts* specials, including *Charlie Brown's All Stars* and *It's the Great Pumpkin, Charlie Brown.* He also appeared in movies such as *Firecreek,* starring Jimmy Stewart and Henry Fonda, and in several popular television series including "Shane." Acting was a family affair in the Shea family—Christopher's younger brother Stephen also appeared in six *Peanuts* specials. I was thrilled to get in touch with Christopher thirty-five years later to talk to him about his memories of *A Charlie Brown Christmas.*

"It always felt like a second family," Christopher said, "working with everyone on all the shows. I especially remember Mr. Melendez howling for the voice of Snoopy. And I recall all the fun that Peter and the rest of us kids had in the studio. When the magazines started writing stories about us, we realized that we were part of something special."

There is no doubt that the high point of the show is Linus reading from the Bible to explain the true meaning of Christmas. I asked Christopher how it felt to be the voice of perhaps the most famous one-minute animation scene ever. "Well, at the time," he said, "being just seven, I didn't realize the depth and perception of what I was reading, even though our family did have deep religious values. From a very early age I remember our whole family listening to the *Messiah* every year as a holiday tradition. But as I grew older I came to appreciate the true meaning of Christmas as it was told on the TV show. And of course it's a thrill now to have my two daughters, who are ten and seven, share this with me and my wife as well as all our relatives and friends. It's definitely a once-in-a-lifetime experience that I will always treasure."

The part of Lucy went to young Hollywood actor Tracy Stratford. A very sweet girl, she impressed us all with her acting skills by stepping up to the mike and turning on the crabbiness in a heartbeat! Tracy set the standard for all the future Lucy's in our shows. She perfectly captured Lucy's

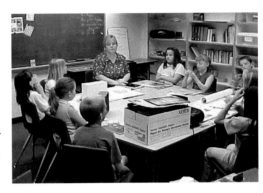

many temperaments—the browbeater who made Charlie Brown miserable, the overly sweet would-be girlfriend of Schroeder, and the goody-goody who was always being grossed-out by Snoopy. We were all amazed at Tracy's versatility and professionalism at such a young age.

The rest of the cast came from my neighborhood in northern California. Sally Dryer played Violet and went on to play Lucy in many of our subsequent specials. The youngest actor, Cathy Steinberg, had just turned six years old when she recorded the part of Charlie Brown's little sister, Sally. Because she was too young to read, we had to feed Cathy one line at a time or, in some cases, just a few words at a time. Chris Doran played Schroeder, Anne Altieri played Frieda, Jeff Ornstein played Pig Pen, and Karen Mendelson (my second cousin) played Patty.

Once the show was broadcast on CBS, the first-, second-, and third-grade cast members became instant celebrities in their schools. Peter Robbins recalled: "Every day a group would come up to me and ask me to say a few words. They would get all excited and say, 'See, that's Charlie Brown!'"

The children who sang the opening and closing songs on the show, "Christmas Time Is Here" and "Hark the Herald Angels Sing," were a group gathered together from a Bay Area church. One of these children, Candace Hackett Shively, is now a teacher in Pennsylvania. When Charles Schulz announced his retirement, she sent him a long, touching letter in which she shared her memories about recording the show:

> *Thirty-four years ago this past September, I raised my hand in a choir rehearsal at St. Paul's Episcopal Church in San Rafael, volunteering for an unnamed task "to help the choir." A*

ABOVE RIGHT: Candace Hackett Shively, now a teacher in Pennsylvania (shown here with her class in May 2000), sang in the children's chorus for *A Charlie Brown Christmas*. She shares the video with her class every year. LEFT: Detail from storyboards by Bill Melendez.

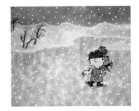

week later I was in the sound studios of Fantasy Records in San Francisco along with five of my fellow choir members, recording the songs for a groundbreaking enterprise, the first animated Peanuts *Christmas special,* A Charlie Brown Christmas. *Mr. Mendelson and all the people at the sound studio were great to us, and I was thrilled to be a twelve-year-old given such an exciting opportunity. We especially enjoyed going out for ice cream afterwards! We went to the studio a couple of times (very late for school nights) and waited to see which of our recordings made the final cut in the December airing of the show.*

Little did I know how much impact that show was to have on my outlook on life, the lives of countless of my students in over twenty years of teaching, and the lives of millions around the world. I cannot listen to the King James version of the Christmas story without hearing Linus's voice adding, ". . . and that's what Christmas is all about, Charlie Brown." I cannot let the day before Christmas vacation pass without sharing the videotape and the story with every class I teach, grades two through eight. Every time I do, the response from each of my students is the same: "That is my very favorite Christmas special. It wouldn't be Christmas without it." To some I have to show the check stub for them to believe that I had the honor of participating in it.

Children were the focus of *A Charlie Brown Christmas,* just as children were always the focus of Sparky's comic strip. There were no adults in the strips and no adults in this first show. In later shows, which included a teacher character, we decided to use a trombone to simulate that voice. Why a trombone? We just thought it was funny.

The cast was recorded, and Bill started the animation process. There are approximately 10,000 drawings in a half hour of animation for a Charlie Brown special. Usually, twelve

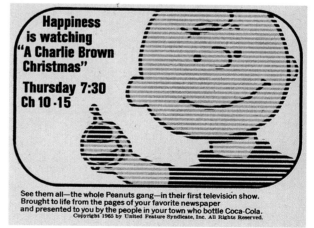

Happiness is watching "A Charlie Brown Christmas" Thursday 7:30 Ch 10·15

See them all—the whole Peanuts gang—in their first television show. Brought to life from the pages of your favorite newspaper and presented to you by the people in your town who bottle Coca-Cola.
Copyright 1965 by United Feature Syndicate, Inc. All Rights Reserved.

24

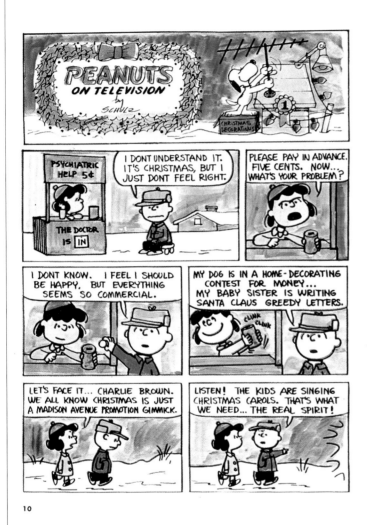

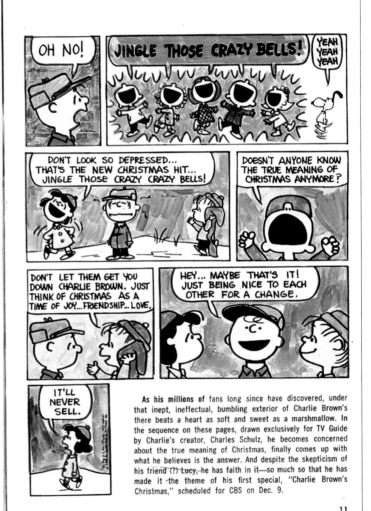

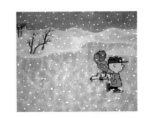

ABOVE: *TV Guide* ran a special "Closeup" feature to announce
the debut of *A Charlie Brown Christmas* in December 1965.
LEFT: An ad for the show that appeared in the same issue.

THE GIFT OF INTROSPECTION

"Christmas is coming, but I'm not happy," Charlie Brown confesses to his best buddy in a scene from *A Charlie Brown Christmas*. " I don't feel the way I'm supposed to feel."

He isn't alone. We've all felt melancholy during the holidays, and we've all been reluctant to say so because that means pondering what the season is all about. That's a tough job for a philosopher or theologian, let alone a sweet little round-headed kid.

Television today favors fast, frequent, exaggerated bursts of action and confrontation. In comparison, *A Charlie Brown Christmas* is almost unnervingly reflective, dependent on words, emotions and small grace notes rather than speed, glitz and noise.

Charlie Brown . . . is America's most-beloved loser, forever falling short of his goals, endlessly stung by failure. Yet he keeps striving, in his own mopey, block-headed way, to become a better person and to make the rest of us better, too.

In the process, he gives his friends, his dog, himself and us an invaluable Christmas gift: the gift of introspection. As we watch the Peanuts gang singing songs around a little tree nobody wanted, we realize that unless we're willing to look inward, to recognize our own selfishness and conquer it, we remain incapable of bringing lasting happiness to others. We remain boxed inside our own preconceptions like beautiful unwrapped presents.

—from "A Charlie Brown Christmas: 30th Anniversary" by Matt Zoller Seitz *Newark Star Ledger*, December 1, 1995

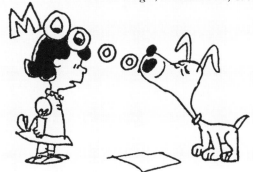

RIGHT: Detail from storyboards by Bill Melendez.

26

drawings are photographed each second, which gives the illusion of movement. Each drawing is initially done in pencil, then copied in ink on an acetate "cel," then painted on the reverse side.

Bill decided to move the characters right off the comic page, with no embellishments, so that the simplicity of Schulz's characters would be retained in animation. Bill's main problem was with Charlie Brown. As he says: "That round head was a real headache. It's very hard to turn a round face." But the rest of the characters presented no problems. In fact, Bill says, Snoopy was the easiest one to draw because he could do so many things.

Toward the end of production, Vince Guaraldi brought in a beautiful opening song. After he laid down the instrumental track, however, we all felt it needed some lyrics. Because we were running out of time, I wrote some lyrics in about fifteen minutes on the back of an envelope. The song became "Christmas Time Is Here," which has become a holiday standard covered by dozens of recording artists. Who knew?

The show was finished a week before the broadcast date. The exhausted staff watched the entire program for the first time. We all felt an uneasiness after the screening. We thought that perhaps we had somehow missed the boat. However, one of the animators, Ed Levitt, stood up in the back row and declared: "*A Charlie Brown Christmas* will run for a hundred years." The rest of us would have settled for two years.

When I flew to New York to present the show to the top two executives at CBS, I was very apprehensive. The three of us screened the program. When the lights came on, the two men looked at each other and then at me, and I could tell instantly that they were disappointed.

"Well, you gave it a good shot," said one. "It seems a little flat . . . a little slow," said the other. I was crushed. "Well," said the first, "we will, of course, air it next week, but I'm afraid we won't be ordering any more. We're sorry; and believe me, we're big *Peanuts* fans. But maybe it's better suited to the comic page."

Then one said to the other, "What should we do with Burgheim?"

"We shouldn't show it to him," said the second.

"Who's Burgheim?" I asked.

"He's the TV writer for *Time* magazine," said one. "He's outside ready to screen the show."

Grasping at straws, I said, "Won't it be worse if we don't show it to him?" They looked at each other for a few seconds and then decided to let him see it. They left and Richard Burgheim came in to the screening room. He watched the show, never said a word, stood up, thanked me, and left the room. I was devastated.

Two days later I flew back to San Francisco, totally despondent. I live a few minutes from the San Francisco airport, and for some reason, the weekly issue of *Time* is always available there on Sunday nights, one day earlier than the Monday deliveries in most of the country. I was literally shaking when I turned to the TV section. To my total surprise and relief, it was a great, positive preview!

I called Sparky and Bill to read them the *Time* article. We were all thrilled. The next day, *TV Guide* gave us a "Closeup" and a two-

LEFT: Original still from the 35mm film.

A SPECIAL THAT REALLY IS SPECIAL

December is the gruelingest month, the time when there seem to be more seasonal "specials" than regular shows on TV. But this Thursday . . . CBS will carry a special that really is special. For one thing, the program is unpretentious; for another, it is unprolonged (30 minutes). Finally, it represents the overdue TV debut of the comic strip *Peanuts*.

A Charlie Brown Christmas stars all the familiar Charles Schulz cartoon characters, faithfully animated by ex-Disney artist Bill Melendez. The parable, too, is pure Schulz. . . . The voices of the characters . . . contribute to the refreshingly low-key tone. . . . *A Charlie Brown Christmas* is one children's special this season that bears repeating.

— from "Security Is a Good Show"
Time, December 10, 1965

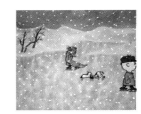

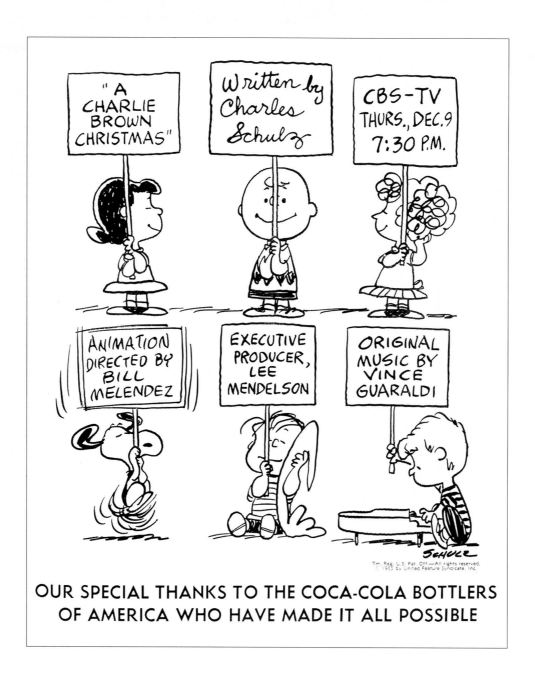

OUR SPECIAL THANKS TO THE COCA-COLA BOTTLERS
OF AMERICA WHO HAVE MADE IT ALL POSSIBLE

page color spread. But, while we finally had some apparent momentum, we had no idea if anyone would actually tune in and watch the first *Peanuts* special when it aired. Shortly after the show aired we heard the exciting news. *A Charlie Brown Christmas* had finished second (to "Bonanza") in the national ratings! CBS called and ordered four more specials, and we suddenly had one of the biggest hits on television.

A few months later, Sparky, Bill, and I found ourselves at the Emmy Awards. *A Charlie Brown Christmas* had been nominated for Best Network Animated Special. We had no thoughts of winning, going up against Walt Disney and many other favorites. In those days the Emmys were presented from New York and Hollywood at the same time. Our category was announced from New York by the fabulous Kukla, Fran, and Ollie. When Ollie Dragon finally said: "And the winner, in Hollywood, is *A Charlie Brown Christmas,*" we were all stunned and had to pull ourselves together to stagger to the stage. Danny Kaye handed us the Emmy and we looked out at all those famous television personalities as if it were a dream. I know we all felt very blessed. And we all realized that poor old Charlie Brown was in show business to stay.

The December 2000 airing of *A Charlie Brown Christmas* marks its 35th consecutive broadcast on CBS-TV. The music from the show has now sold over four million records, having been recorded by David Benoit, Wynton Marsalis, George Winston, and many others. All

---

MOVE OVER, RED!

The Nielsen ratings reported that *A Charlie Brown Christmas* was the second most popular show on television when it debuted on the evening of December 9, 1965. We were thrilled to have such a big success in a very competitive prime time slot. The show has aired on CBS every year since.

LATEST TOP TEN PROGRAMS
(as announced in *Advertising Age*, January 10, 1966)

	Number of Homes Viewing
1. Bonanza (NBC)	17,650,000
2. Charlie Brown (CBS)	15,490,000
3. Red Skelton (CBS)	14,470,000
4. Danny Thomas (NBC) *Tie*	14,420,000
4. Lucy Show (CBS) *Tie*	14,420,000
6. Walt Disney (NBC)	14,260,000
7. Gomer Pyle (CBS)	14,040,000
8. Andy Griffith (CBS)	13,610,000
9. Man from U.N.C.L.E. (NBC) *Tie*	13,340,000
9. Beverly Hillbillies (CBS) *Tie*	13,340,000

LEFT: The announcement ad for *A Charlie Brown Christmas* that appeared on December 8, 1965, in the *Hollywood Reporter* and *Daily Variety*.

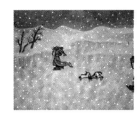

"A CHARLIE BROWN CHRISTMAS"

THANKS TO VIEWERS FOR A 45% SHARE AND THANKS TO THE CRITICS INCLUDING:

TIME MAGAZINE:

" 'Happiness' is Charlie Brown — animated. CHARLIE BROWN'S CHRISTMAS is a special that is really special — one that bears repeating."

HOLLYWOOD REPORTER:

"...delightfully novel and amusing..."

NEW YORK WORLD - TELEGRAM, Harriet Van Horne:

"... if you missed Charlie's debut on TV, I'm sorry for you. Write CBS and say all you want for Christmas is a repeat ... Linus reading the story of the Nativity was, quite simply, the dramatic highlight of the season ..."

U.P.I., Rick DuBrow:

"... the Peanuts characters last night staked out a claim to a major television future..."

WASHINGTON POST, Lawrence Laurent:

"... natural-born loser Charlie Brown finally turned up a real winner last night ... excellent animation ... fine job of matching voices to characters..."

WEEKLY VARIETY:

"... fascinating and haunting..."

PHILADELPHIA INQUIRER, Harry Harris:

"... Charlie Brown's Christmas is a yule classic ... it generated quiet warmth and amusement ..."

SAN FRANCISCO CHRONICLE, Terrence O'Flaherty:

"... Charlie Brown was a gem of a television show ... the script was right ... the voices of the children were a delight ..."

NEW YORK DAILY NEWS, Ben Gross:

"... charm and good taste marked the animated Charlie Brown show ... it appealed to grownups as well as the moppet set ..."

NEW YORK POST, Bob Williams:

"... very neat transition from comic page to screen..."

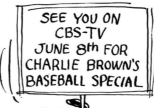

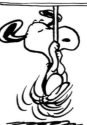

SEE YOU ON CBS-TV JUNE 8th FOR CHARLIE BROWN'S BASEBALL SPECIAL

A LEE MENDELSON—BILL MELENDEZ PRODUCTION

Our thanks to the Coca-Cola Co., McCann-Erickson, Inc. CBS-TV, United Feature Syndicate, Inc., Ashley Famous Agency, Inc. and to Charles Schulz and to Vince Guaraldi.

BOB, BING AND CHARLIE BROWN

In the sixties and seventies, before the cable and satellite age, there were only three networks and *A Charlie Brown Christmas* held a vast percentage of the television viewing audience. When the ratings revealed that we were right up at there with Bob Hope and Bing Crosby, we were proud to be in such good company.

ALL–TIME TOP 10 CHRISTMAS RATINGS

	RATING	YEAR
Bob Hope Christmas Special (NBC)	46.6	1970
Bob Hope Christmas Special (NBC)	45.0	1971
Bob Hope Christmas Special (NBC)	38.5	1969
Bob Hope Christmas Special (NBC)	38.0	1967
Bob Hope Christmas Special (NBC)	36.3	1968
Bob Hope Christmas Special (NBC)	35.5	1966
A CHARLIE BROWN CHRISTMAS (CBS)	34.8	1969
Christmas with The Bing Crosbys (NBC)	34.3	1972
A CHARLIE BROWN CHRISTMAS (CBS)	34.3	1967
Bob Hope Christmas Special (NBC)	34.1	1972

three of those musicians told me that they grew up listening to the Vince Guaraldi music, which had a tremendous effect on the development of their careers.

Charles Schulz told me years ago: "There will always be a market for innocence in this country," and fortunately, he was right. Sparky's core values were the foundation of *A Charlie Brown Christmas*, and his core values are what America is still all about.

You were a good man, Charles Schulz, and we've been honored by the pleasure of your company, your humor, your faith, and your dedication to the meaningful elements of American society.

LEFT: A second announcement ad ran in the trade magazines after the debut of the show, filled with glowing reviews from publications throughout the country. RIGHT: Charles Schulz and Lee Mendelson in 1998.

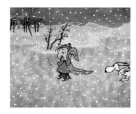

charles m. schulz,
all-american

the gentle,
straightforward message of *A Charlie Brown Christmas* tackles a big issue with little strokes. In that half hour, Charlie Brown faces the frustration of a commercialized Christmas and is gently reminded of the real meaning of the holiday. The show combines the questioning and faith that somehow coexist within people everywhere, and perfectly illuminates the inner life of Charles M. Schulz.

An optimist, great patriot, and deeply spiritual man, Schulz also suffered from self-doubt and was genuinely amazed at the outpouring of affection he received from around the world after announcing his retirement in late 1999. The success of the *Peanuts* strip, *A Charlie Brown Christmas,* and all the television specials that followed lies in Schulz's ability to express both the light and dark sides of life without letting go of childlike innocence. "On the surface," wrote *Doonesbury* creator Gerry Trudeau, "Schulz's message was filled with a uniquely American sense of optimism—'Li'l Folks' with big dreams, never giving up, always trudging out to the mound one more time. But the pain of sustaining that hope showed everywhere."

Comic strips made their mark on Charles Schulz from the very beginning. At two days old, his uncle nicknamed him "Sparky" in honor of Sparkplug, Barney Google's horse in the very popular comic strip. As early as kindergarten, Schulz was given a glimmer of things to come when his teacher looked at his first drawing and said, "Someday, Charles, you're going to be an artist."

The son of a barber and housewife in St. Paul, Minnesota, Schulz had two loves during his school years: cartooning and golf. He was painfully shy and not fond of school—even the art classes. Frustrated by all the planning and preparation the art teachers demanded, he preferred to sit down with a clean piece of paper, get down to business, and create a cartoon in a half hour. On top of his dislike for the way art class was taught, he felt intimated by the other students, whom he felt had more talent. He once told an interviewer that his fear of not measuring up drove him to study art through a correspondence course after graduating from high school. "I was afraid to go to art school," he said, "because I'd be right back where I was in

LEFT: Sparky is filmed driving his children to school in Lee Mendelson's 1963 documentary, *A Boy Named Charlie Brown.*

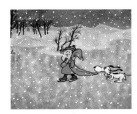

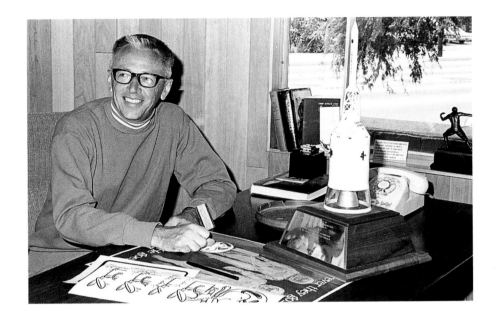

high school—in a class with a lot of people who could draw better than I could. And I'd be a nobody again."

This sense of alienation, personified in Charlie Brown, is one of the deeply personal yet universally shared feelings that Charles Schulz infused into each of the *Peanuts* characters. With simplicity and wit he pioneered new ground in comics with characters that reflect all the insecurity, anxiety, and joy of being human. Garry Trudeau recognizes *Peanuts* as a strip that "vibrated with '50s alienation" and broke new ground in the art form. He defines Schulz's work as the "gold standard" for cartoonists; a strip that "was populated with complicated, neurotic characters speaking smart, haiku-perfect dialogue."

The *Peanuts* characters are based on Schulz's childhood memories as well as on observations of people close to him. Charlie Brown's round, ordinary face represents Schulz's child-

ABOVE: Sparky, on a visit to NASA's NCRC space division in Newbury Park, California, in 1968. Snoopy and Charlie Brown were chosen by NASA as mascots and promotional characters in the 1960s, and an award program was initiated to acknowledge outstanding performance with a "Silver Snoopy" award (a NASA program that continues to this day). *Peanuts* went into orbit when the Apollo 10 lunar module was named Snoopy and the command module named Charlie Brown. LEFT: Original still from the 35mm film.

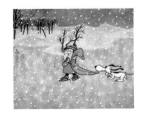

hood impression of his own plain, bland looks. He felt almost invisible in his ordinariness, and drew Charlie Brown with the simple, indistinct features of an "everyman." The origins of Lucy's personality were also drawn from Schulz himself as well as from his children. He once described his first daughter, Meredith, as a "fussbudget" like Lucy, and pointed out that he went through a period of expressing a lot of Lucy-like sarcasm. "This strip gives me an outlet because there was a time in my life when I didn't know that sarcasm was not a good trait to have, and I have overcome this," he told an interviewer in 1968. The idea for Linus and his blanket came from Schulz's first three children, who each dragged blankets around the house. Reflecting on the first appearance of Linus and his blanket in the 1950s, Schulz wrote, "I did not know then that the term 'security blanket' would later become part of the American language."

Snoopy was based on the artist's boyhood dog, Spike, a black-and-white mixed breed who loved to ride in the car, could understand about 50 words, and ate everything in sight—from tacks and pins to rubber balls and razor blades. Schulz drew a picture of Spike and submitted it to RIPLEY'S BELIEVE IT OR NOT! with a description of the amazing things the dog ate. The piece was printed in the nationally syndicated column and became Schulz's first published drawing. Next to the drawing, the credit read, "Drawn by 'Sparky.'"

After high school, Sparky was determined to get his cartoons published. In spite of a letterbox full of rejection slips, he persisted in submitting his work to all the major magazines —until the war intervened. Schulz served in the army for three years during World War II, marching through France and Germany as an infantryman. When his tour of duty was over, he returned to Minnesota and resumed his cartooning while working as a letterer for the Catholic comic magazine *Timeless Topix* and as an instructor for his fondly remembered correspondence course, the Art Instruction Schools. During these years Sparky's ambition and persistence began to pay off—fifteen of his cartoons were published in the *Saturday Evening Post,* and he launched a weekly cartoon feature in the *St. Paul Pioneer Press*. The fulfillment of his dreams came in 1950, when he signed with the United Feature Syndicate. He hoped the name of his strip, *Li'l Folks*, would remain the same in syndication, but a United Feature executive decided to name the cartoon *Peanuts*.

In spite of their new and, according to Schulz, somewhat baffling title, the pint-sized cast of characters he had been developing for years began a new life in a daily strip that ran in seven newspapers. In two years *Peanuts* was so popular that Schulz published his first book of cartoons, and in 1955 he received honorable recognition from his peers with his first National Cartoonists Society Reuben Award. By December 1965, when *A Charlie Brown Christmas* brought *Peanuts* to television for the very first time, Schulz was becoming a household name. Charlie Brown, Linus, Lucy, Snoopy and the rest of the *Peanuts* gang were well on their way to becoming permanent icons of American popular culture.

After seven decades of drawing, the creator of the most popular comic strip of all time announced the retirement of the *Peanuts* strip in December 1999. Charles M. Schulz died peacefully in his sleep on February 12, 2000, just hours before the Sunday papers ran his last cartoon.

After creating 45 television specials, four feature films, and 18 Saturday morning shows with Sparky, producer Lee Mendelson and animator Bill Melendez look back on their careers with their good friend and the background of making *A Charlie Brown Christmas.* —*Ed.*

What is it about* A Charlie Brown Christmas *that has made it such an enduring classic? What does the show say about Charles M. Schulz?

BILL MELENDEZ: This little story and the way it's told is almost as simple and direct as Sparky's cartoon strip. The message is so gentle, there's nothing pompous about the story. It was amazing how Sparky came up with the religious aspect of the story and made it so acceptable. He wanted to be very straightforward and honest, and he said what he wanted to say because he was a very religious guy. When I first looked at that part of the

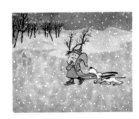

story I told Sparky, "We can't do this, it's too religious. And he said to me, "Bill, if we don't do it, who else can? We're the only ones who can do it." I wasn't convinced that was true at the time, but he was right about so many things. It just didn't sound right for a cartoon, an entertainment. When I read that part, I thought we were going to kill this thing, but by golly he came through.

In this and every show, Sparky always stuck in a little message.

LEE MENDELSON: My reaction to the religious aspect of the story was that it was something new—there hadn't been any animation, to the best of my knowledge, drawn from the Bible. I didn't think too much about it. I trusted Sparky's instincts. We were trying to do a comedy and this seemed serious for that, but I trusted him. This show contains the midwestern values and tastes of Charles Schulz, both religious and musical.

I think another reason *A Charlie Brown Christmas* was so successful was because of the rich variety of music. You had Beethoven, Felix Mendelssohn, religious music, and jazz. That music permeated the whole show. Another element that made it different was that, up until then, adults had done the kids' voices in animation. This was one of the first times that kids did the voices.

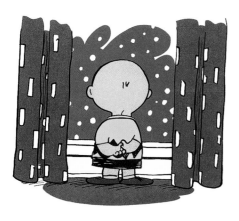

BILL MELENDEZ: A big part of Sparky's personality comes through in *A Charlie Brown Christmas*. I thought that Schulz was what they call a true Christian gentleman, a genuinely nice person. He was very religious, a student of the Bible, and he taught adult Bible classes.

Sometimes he would just do a very nice thing. I remember one mutual friend of ours, a publishing person, who suddenly had a lot of problems in his life. Everything happened to him: his wife died, he lost his job, he couldn't even get around Los Angeles because he had always had a company car. Immediately, without saying anything, Sparky bought a nice car and gave it to him. And I'm sure he must have done other things, too, that none of us knows about.

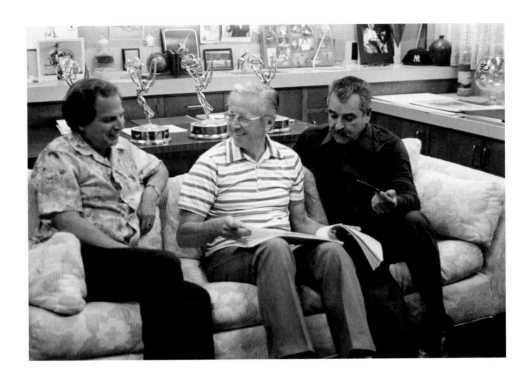

LEE MENDELSON: Sparky and his wife, Jeannie, were extremely philanthropic. He was probably the most philanthropic man I ever met and he never talked about it. One of his other great characteristics was loyalty. Whenever someone tried to get in the way of Lee Mendelson or Bill Melendez, he stopped them cold. He was extremely loyal and expected loyalty in return. Although we had creative disagreements from time to time—anyone's going to have that—over the 37 years we all got along and had a good time. That's a nice thing to know, that you're not going to have some big studio come in and take over. No matter what studio called him, no matter how famous the people involved, he would always say, "Call Bill and Lee." Loyalty in general is hard to come by, and in this business it's very rare.

ABOVE: Sparky looks over a set of storyboards with executive producer Lee Mendelson, left, and director/animator Bill Melendez, right. Behind them are four of the seven Emmys the trio received for their *Peanuts* television specials.

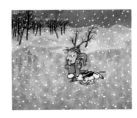

Like all of us, Sparky had different sides. The low-key, shy man you saw in public was the way he was when sitting around with a few colleagues or friends, but inside was this other person; very creative, very aggressive, very competitive. Even diametrically opposed, these traits were part of him, and we're all complex like that.

Because of our age differences, Sparky was like a big brother to me and a little brother to Bill. This helped us work well together, too, because we each brought something different to the table. Our different ages and backgrounds were strong points in building great teamwork. We worked very well together on this first television special, and things only got better throughout the years.

Bill and I discovered that we may have a collaboration in our family histories, which is very interesting. My great-great-grandfather sold clothing to miners in San Francisco in 1850 and 1851. I'm a third-generation San Franciscan. And Bill's great-grandfather sold mules to the miners in San Francisco. So they might have known each other. The Mendelson-Melendez collaboration may go back to 1851.

BILL MELENDEZ: Regarding working with Sparky, we respected each other's area of expertise and got comfortable with each other. He lived up in Sebastopol in northern California and I lived down in Los Angeles, so we didn't get under each other's feet or on each other's nerves.

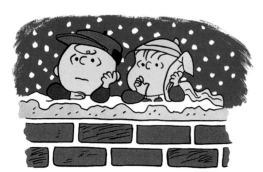

It worked. We didn't have to be together every day to do *A Charlie Brown Christmas* or any of the other shows. He realized that animation was a completely different field than comic strips, and he was happy to not really be involved in the motion picture industry.

LEE MENDELSON: He would simply say, "Here's the story, go do it." We only got together once every few months, but it was always fun. Seeing each other every couple of months was like friends getting together, which we were.

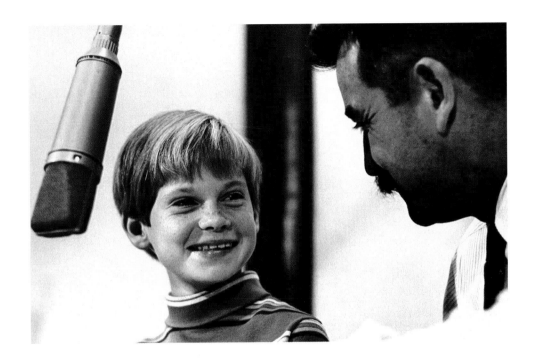

What was one of your responsibilities in working with the children in the studio for **A Charlie Brown Christmas?**

BILL MELENDEZ: I'm the one who had to read the lines to the children, including the little actor playing Linus. He was too young to read. Sparky and I had a long-running joke about my accent, and I told him, "Sparky, this kid is going to read this scene in a Spanish accent and it's going to sound terrible!" Working with those very young children was a challenge, but it was a lot of fun. It's hard to direct these kids. This is where Schulz was smart; he let us do it. Once he got us started he left us alone.

ABOVE: Sally Dryer, who played Violet in *A Charlie Brown Christmas,* in the recording studio with director Bill Melendez. Sally played the roles of Lucy, Sophie, and other characters in a number of *Peanuts* specials.

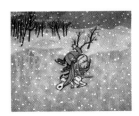

In your many years with Schulz, did you find similarities between him and his **Peanuts** *characters?*

LEE MENDELSON: He said to me once, "Charlie Brown is the way I am and Snoopy is the way I wish I could be." That was his summary.

In the first documentary we made about Sparky, in 1963, he talks about being promoted two grades when he was in elementary school. So suddenly he's the youngest, the skinniest, and the smallest in his class and they all picked on him. This is where Charlie Brown was born. It came right out of his childhood.

BILL MELENDEZ: I always saw similarities between Sparky and his characters. After we did some animation together, I found that he was able to develop his attitude about Snoopy and bring him out even more. For example, before *A Charlie Brown Christmas,* Snoopy was very limited in what he could do. And suddenly he was involved in airplanes. He could simulate flying a plane and go up and do everything. Now that expanded the scope of Snoopy's use. He became extremely valuable to Schulz in that his whole life opened up. He could use gags that were never used before. He used to limit Snoopy to being a dog—he was like a real dog in the earlier years—but eventually he became much more.

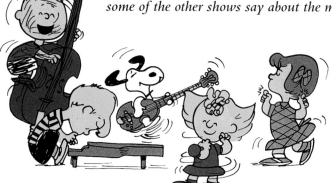

If **A Charlie Brown Christmas** *reveals Sparky's religious values and his musical tastes, what do some of the other shows say about the man?*

LEE MENDELSON: First of all, he was very proud of his service in World War II. So proud that we went back 25 years after the war and went to all the places he had served, to make a documentary for PBS called *To Remember.* He took us through France and visited many of the places where he and his battalion had come through. We also did a show called *What Have We Learned, Charlie Brown?*, which was a tribute to the

44

men who died in World War I and World War II, and we also did a series called *This Is America, Charlie Brown*, which is eight shows on U.S. history. Whenever I had conversations with Sparky, he said he loved this country. In his television interview for "60 Minutes" in 1999, he said that he had no concern or fears about this country because the common man, the working man in this country is so solid, so patriotic, and so good that the great majority will always prevail. He was very optimistic about the United States.

Sparky was very competitive—whether it was golf, tennis, Ping-Pong, or billiards, he always wanted to win, but not in an unpleasant way. He liked to win, there's no doubt about it. He was a good athlete; an excellent golfer, a pretty good tennis player and a very good pool player. When he drew his *Peanuts* characters playing sports, he was very particular about getting the details right and his knowledge of sports came through. He was also a great conversationalist. He loved to sit around and talk more than anything else. He and I drove from San Francisco to Los Angeles once and talked nonstop for seven hours.

Sparky would always ask people, whether a priest, a hockey player, or an animator, all about what they did and why they did it. He

"He said that he had no concern or fears about this country because the common man, the working man in this country is so solid, so patriotic, and so good that the great majority will always prevail. He was very optimistic about the United States."

—Lee Mendelson

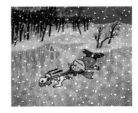

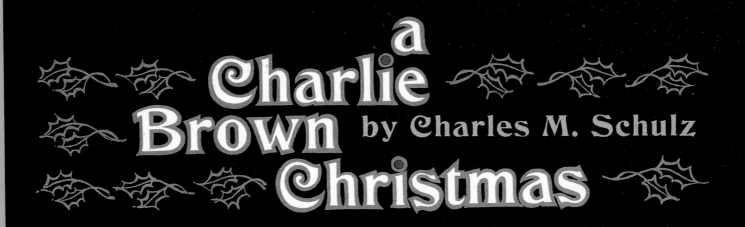

a Charlie Brown Christmas

by Charles M. Schulz

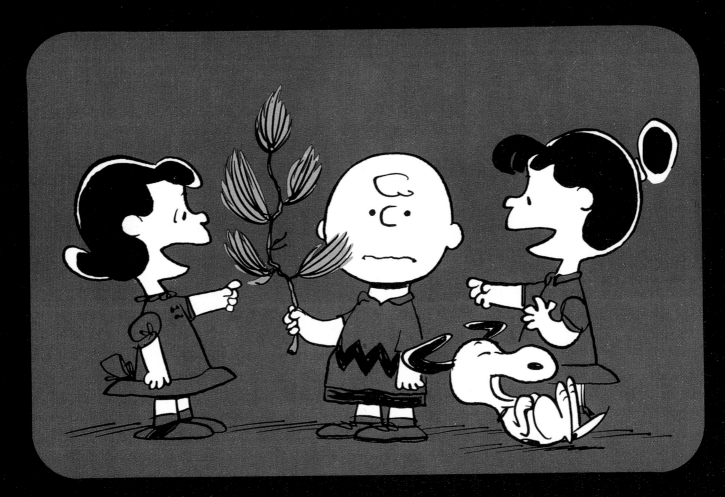

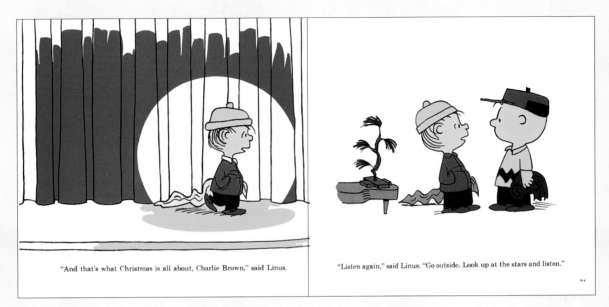

"And that's what Christmas is all about, Charlie Brown," said Linus.

"Listen again," said Linus. "Go outside. Look up at the stars and listen."

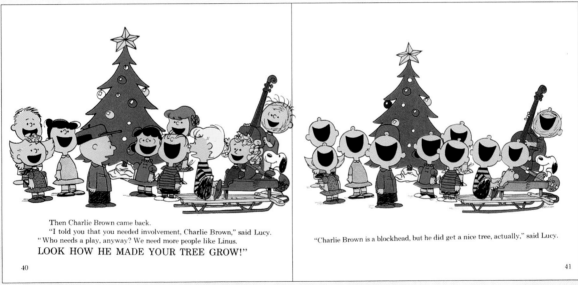

Then Charlie Brown came back.
"I told you that you needed involvement, Charlie Brown," said Lucy.
"Who needs a play, anyway? We need more people like Linus.
LOOK HOW HE MADE YOUR TREE GROW!"

40

"Charlie Brown is a blockhead, but he did get a nice tree, actually," said Lucy.

41

The television special was adapted as a picture storybook (cover, left) published by The World Publishing Company in 1965. Before the era of the home video, this book made it possible for fans to enjoy the story throughout the holiday season.

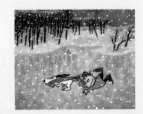

was very interested in everyone's profession. I thought that was fascinating because so few people do that; they want to talk about what they do. He never talked about what he did, he always would ask, "Where did you grow up? Why are you in this field?" And people really were touched by that, that he would take the time to do that.

He loved the movies. He loved stage plays and he read voraciously. I think he read one or two books a week. And he loved all kinds of music. So when you're going to movies, going to stage shows and reading books and listening to music all the time, you've got a well-rounded foundation. Not only was he interested in talking to people, he got ideas from talking to people. Part of it was research and development for him.

They asked the president of Sony if he could sum up in one word why he'd been so successful, and he said, "Yes: curiosity." And I think you can sum up Charles Schulz with the word curiosity. He was curious about everything in life and that curiosity ended up in the comic strip and in the television shows. I really think that's an important insight to who he was.

How was Sparky regarded by his peers, and how did he handle the enormous popularity of his work?

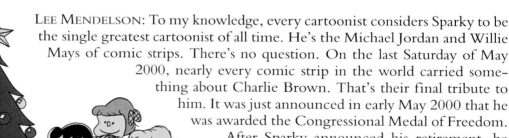

LEE MENDELSON: To my knowledge, every cartoonist considers Sparky to be the single greatest cartoonist of all time. He's the Michael Jordan and Willie Mays of comic strips. There's no question. On the last Saturday of May 2000, nearly every comic strip in the world carried something about Charlie Brown. That's their final tribute to him. It was just announced in early May 2000 that he was awarded the Congressional Medal of Freedom.

After Sparky announced his retirement, he was absolutely flabbergasted by the outpouring of letters, phone calls, and messages he received. He was overwhelmed by the public affection. He may have always hoped for it, he may have thought it was there, but he didn't have any idea. I was with him a lot in those months, and I often heard him look at his piles of mail and say, "I can't believe it." Whether it was a letter from the president of the United States or one of the millions of his readers, his surprise was very genuine. So I guess at heart he wasn't quite sure what the public thought.

Sparky was very proud of *A Charlie Brown Christmas*, very proud of the stage shows, very proud that "security blanket" was put in the dictionary. They once asked him what his philosophy was, and he said, "My philosophy is to be sure to get the strip to the post office on time." He did not consider himself a deep philosopher at all, although he was called a philosopher. Some people put labels on him that he never accepted. He always said, "I draw funny pictures. Nothing more, nothing less."

"He did not consider himself a deep philosopher at all, although he was called a philosopher. Some people put labels on him that he never accepted. He always said, 'I draw funny pictures. Nothing more, nothing less."

—Lee Mendelson

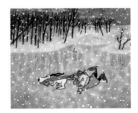

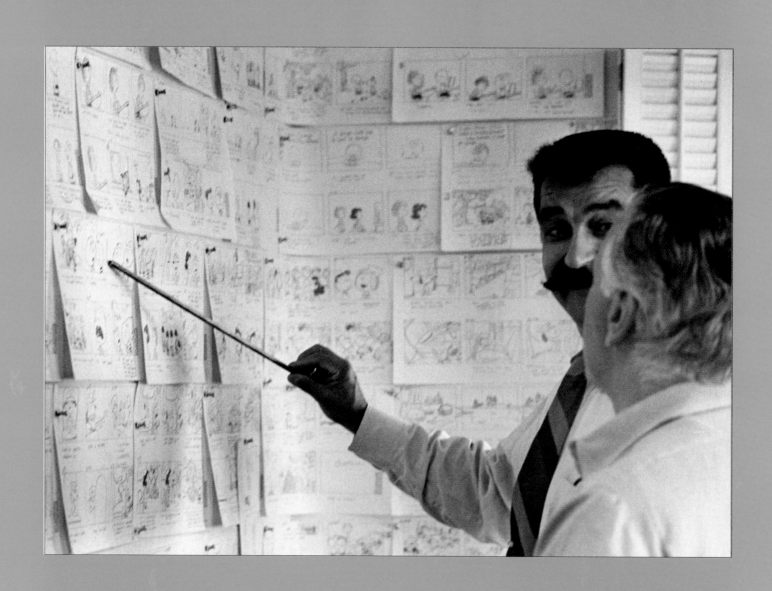

bill melendez, animation artist

born in Hermosillo, Mexico, in 1916, Bill Melendez grew up in Arizona and California and began his animation career with The Walt Disney studio in 1938. There he worked on feature-length animated films such as *Pinocchio* and *Bambi,* as well as many short Mickey Mouse and Donald Duck cartoons. Through most of the 1940s he worked at the Warner Bros. Cartoons studio, animating short subjects featuring Bugs Bunny, Daffy Duck, and Porky Pig. From these major animation studios Melendez moved on to directing industrial films, television productions, and commercials, garnering hundreds of awards including three Art Director's Medals and critical acclaim at the Cannes, Edinburgh, and Venice Film festivals. He has won eight Emmy Awards, the first of which was for *A Charlie Brown Christmas*. He holds the record as the world's most prolific director of animated television commercials, having created more than 1,000 spots.

Ever since his first collaboration with Charles Schulz on a Ford commercial in 1959, Bill Melendez has been the only animator permitted to work with the *Peanuts* characters. He is the sole animator for every *Peanuts* ad, such as the familiar MetLife and Hallmark campaigns, every television special and cartoon, and each theatrical production. A Hollywood institution in his own right, Melendez remains actively at work in the production company he founded in Los Angeles in 1964.

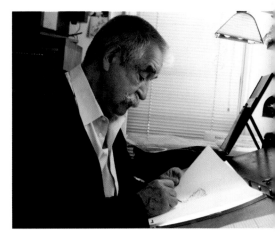

Charles Schulz never sought out or even considered using any other animator in more than three decades, which speaks volumes for the quality of Bill Melendez's work. Their creative partnership brought a new dimension to the *Peanuts* gang that will live on in beloved television specials such as *A Charlie Brown Christmas* for many generations to come. —*Ed.*

LEFT: Bill points out a scene in a storyboard sequence in his studio, 1970.
RIGHT: Bill Melendez at his desk, 1999. A Hollywood institution, Bill's career spans the golden age of Disney and Warner cartoons in the 1930s and 1940s to the *Peanuts* anniversary television special *Here's to You, Charlie Brown: 50 Great Years!* which aired in May 2000. He has also created more than 1,000 animated commercials, making him the world's most prolific director in that field.

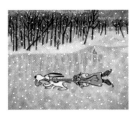

When did you first meet Sparky?

I was doing a lot of commercial work for the advertising agency J. Walter Thompson. One of their biggest accounts was the Ford Motor Company. I used to go to their offices in New York quite a bit and was doing a lot of animation for their commercials, so we got kind of friendly. One day one of the executives asked me, "How would you like to audition for a job?" I said, "I'm an animator, we don't audition!" But he told me that it was a very special client and I'd have to audition. He asked me if I'd ever heard of a comic strip called *Peanuts*. I knew the strip and I thought it was a very nice comic with good stories.

This executive told me that Ford wanted to use *Peanuts* animation in its television commercials for their new car, the Falcon. They came up with *Peanuts* during a meeting with the head of the advertising agency, Norman Strauss, whose little granddaughter was running around the room. She overheard them talking about finding a character or a spokesman, and she piped up, "Grandpa, why don't you use *Peanuts*?" Old Strauss asked one of his executives what the heck she was talking about and they explained the popular strip to him. He agreed to check it out, and they contacted Schulz. Sparky was hesitant about commercializing the strip at first. Then the agency approached him in a gentler way. They asked, "We just wondered, if you'd be all right with it, could you say a few nice words about the Ford Motor Company and about Ford cars." Schulz said, "Sure, I don't mind doing that because the only car I've ever driven was a Ford."

They told Schulz they had an animator they'd like him to meet, so a Thompson executive and I went up to Schulz's home in Sebastopol, California, to meet him. He had a real nice little estate, about 26 acres of redwood in rolling hills. His house was in a place called Coffee Lane and he called his home the Coffee Grounds. He had a sign up when we arrived that said WELCOME NEW YORK, WELCOME HOLLYWOOD.

Sparky wanted to know what I did, so I showed him my reel of commercials. He must have liked it, because he agreed to try me out and do

52

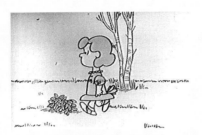

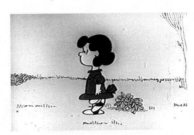

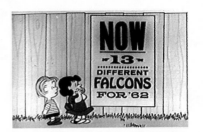

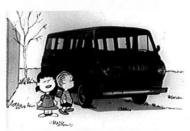

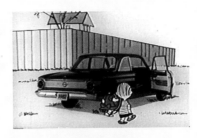

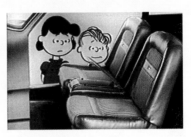

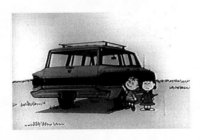

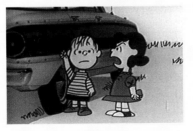

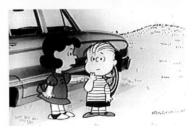

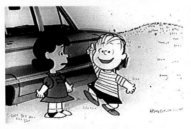

The very first *Peanuts* animation was created by Bill Melendez for a Ford Motor Company television commercial campaign in the early 1960s. Ford chose the Peanuts characters to introduce Americans to its new model, the Falcon. These stills are from two commercials that aired in 1962.

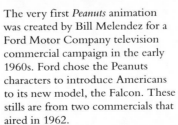

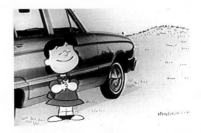

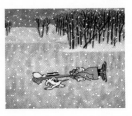

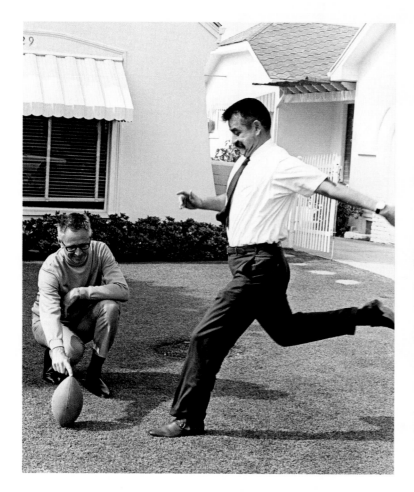 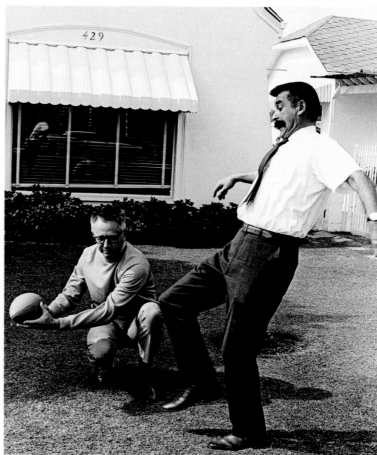

Sparky and Bill play out the Lucy and Charlie Brown
football gag.

the one-minute Falcon commercial. A few weeks later he came down to Hollywood to the studio where I was working and I brought out the spot in a stack of drawings about eight inches high. Sparky said, "What's that?" I told him it was the commercial. He said, "My goodness, I don't make that many drawings in a year!" He picked up the first drawing on the top of the stack and looked at it. "That's pretty good," he said. Then he picked up the next one. "Not as good, but still okay." Then he lifted up the third drawing and said, "That's a terrible drawing. No, that's not acceptable." I handed him a pencil and said, "Here you are Mr. Schulz, you draw Snoopy in that position." He said, "I never draw him in that position." I explained to him that in animation we have to turn Snoopy and the other characters around at times, which entails drawing the figure in an unfamiliar position for a fleeting, one-sixth of a second. Once he saw all the drawings in action, he understood the process and wasn't worried about his characters losing their original look.

What was your next collaboration with Sparky?

After the two first Ford spots in 1962, Sparky recommended me for the animation in Lee Mendelson's documentary about him. This is the two-minute spot of animation that came to the attention of Coca-Cola and led to the production of *A Charlie Brown Christmas* for CBS.

What was the difference between this kind of animation and the work you did for studios such as Disney and Warner Bros.?

I finally figured out how to turn Snoopy, Charlie Brown, and the other characters to hide the fact that these were really flat designs and not three-dimensional. At Disney and at every other studio in those years, we always animated three-dimensional characters. With that first commercial came my chance to animate a cartoon design, a flat design, which I had always wanted to do, and it was perfect.

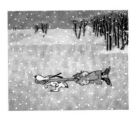

I had to animate Sparky's characters in such a way that you wouldn't see the turns. I found ways of animating this and hiding the fact that scope of the movement was very limited. Charlie Brown has this big head and tiny arms; he could never scratch the top of his head. So I found out that you had to do things like move his hand to the top of his head in profile, for example, then you could make his arm as long as you want. Snoopy saved me because Snoopy is more like a real animated character. He can do anything—move and dance—and he's very easy to animate, whereas the kids are nearly impossible! I've always had to think quickly and learn how to cope with the limitations of the design.

In addition to animating the shows, you have always been the "voice" of Snoopy. How did this happen?

We had to come up with a solution for making Snoopy "talk" in the animated shows, and my first suggestion was to use the voice of a crazy friend of mine who could talk in a high-pitched, cartoonish voice. I taped him speaking a lot of Snoopy's dialogue from the strip and sent it to Schulz. He laughed and said it was pretty good, but told me we couldn't use it. "Snoopy's a dog and he can't talk," he said. Then I decided to speak the lines and we sped it up on the tape. It was funny and it didn't sound like talking at all. I made that tape as a demonstration to show an actor what I wanted him to do, but we were running out of production time and the editor told me that we had to fill in Snoopy's dialogue or we couldn't finish the picture. I told him to just use the tape I made myself, and everybody accepted that crazy dog talk. Now I also do the sound for Woodstock.

ABOVE LEFT: Bill, right, reviews a film with his staff at his studio in Los Angeles. BELOW LEFT: Sandy Claxton, one of Bill's production assistants, works on an exposure sheet that details the timing of each scene in an animated film.

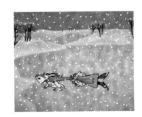

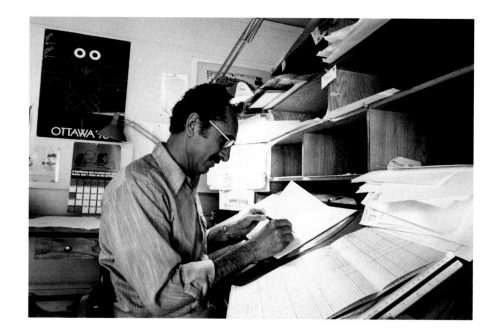

Sparky didn't want any adult voices in the films, either, so we came up with the idea of using a trombone. In the recording studio, an actor would read the line to the trombone player using a lot of inflections in his voice. The trombone player would then play and shape the musical line to mimic the inflections of the actor's voice.

Did you have any other creative input in A Charlie Brown Christmas *and the other animated films?*

Sparky and I worked very closely on the stories for the television shows, the commercials, and everything else. To begin, he would send me an outline and I worked from that, filling in the text. Then I'd send him storyboards and he would change and rewrite. Every story would go back and forth between us in that way.

ABOVE: Animator Sam Jaimes at work in the Bill Melendez studio.

What made it easy to work with Sparky was that he established our roles from the very start, saying, "I'm a cartoon strip artist and you're an animator. You can't do my cartoon strips and I can't do your animation. Therefore, if you do your job well and I do my job well, everything will work." We got along very well that way. Once he gave me an outline for the story he was doing next, I would see him twice to complete it. We'd have two two-hour meetings. After the second one, when I thought we had a complete story, I'd send it back to Sparky one more time and he'd correct all the English. He was very intent on using perfect English, of course.

What was your reaction when learning that you had six months to create* A Charlie Brown Christmas? *Was that a realistic deadline?

It wasn't crazy to have a six-month deadline. The network talked about doing an hour-long show at one point, but Lee and I were both against it and we convinced them to make it a half-hour program. Actually, by the time we really got going on the show, there were only four months left. For a half-hour show, that was still okay.

I thought an hour was too long for ani-

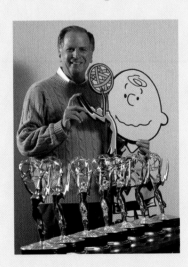

A CHARLIE BROWN CHRISTMAS AWARDS

EMMY AWARD
*for Best Network
Animated Special, 1965*

PEABODY BROADCASTING AWARD
*for Outstanding Children's
and Youth's Program, 1965*

Lee Mendelson with the *Peanuts* Emmys.

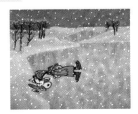

1ST

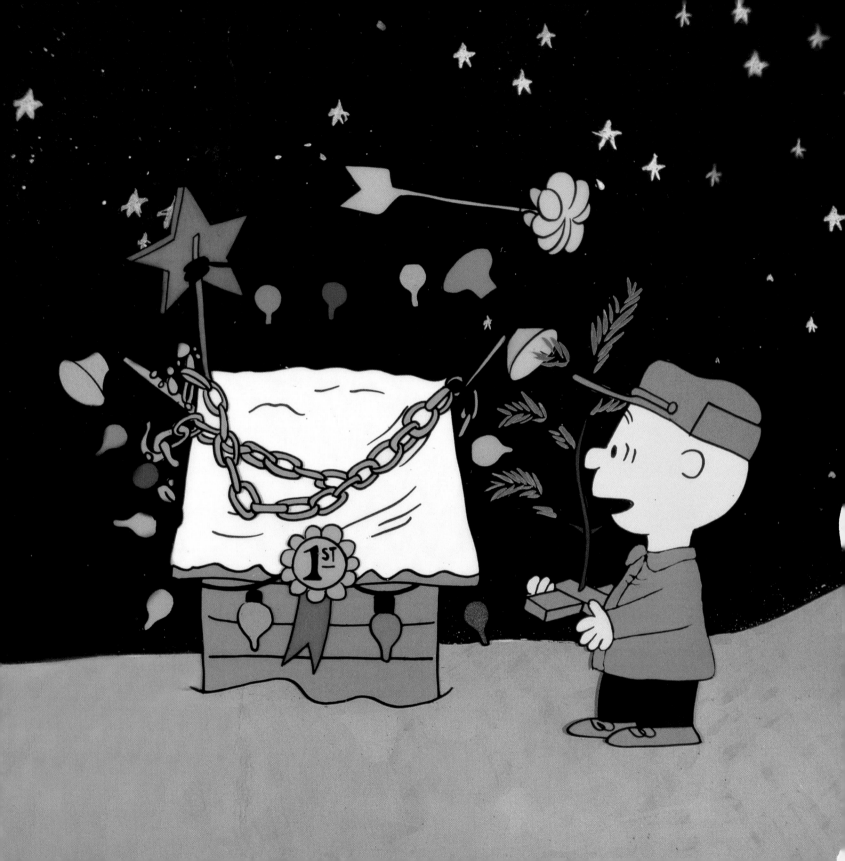

mation for more reasons than just the production time involved. I've always felt it's wrong to project an hour of animation on television, because of the stress it puts on the eyes. The television signal fluctuates at a cycle of 60 times per second, so the nerve endings in your eyes get tired. My theory was and still is that extended animation is okay for film viewing but not television. There's no cycle on film, but on television, everything is split up too much. When you put animation through the TV, the cycle is too fast.

How did you feel about seeing the final version of **A Charlie Brown Christmas** *just before it aired in December, 1965?*

When we saw the finished show, we thought we had killed it. It had so many warts and bumps and lumps and things. A year later we fixed up a few things, but we never completely re-created the show. The inconsistencies and little problems seem to make it even more endearing to a lot of people, and Sparky never wanted to change it.

Lee Mendelson says that Sparky was very happy with your work because you never tried to change his characters or his style. In Lee's words, "The genius of this whole thing is that Bill moved the comic strip, and that's all he did, he didn't embellish it. He didn't make thicker lines or make it fancier. He moved what was there, and that was the trick." How did you approach Sparky's style?

I didn't try to Disney-fy it. Sparky understood that we didn't want to take his characters away from him. We didn't want to change them, just to make his characters work—*his* characters. So he came to trust me on that.

LEFT: Charlie Brown tries to decorate his little tree in this original cel from the show.

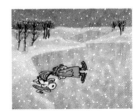

SC.42

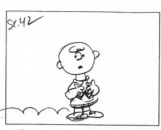

C.BROWN WALKS TO STAGE CTR & FACES KIDS

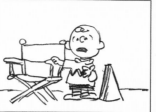

C.B: "WELL, IT'S REEL GOOD SEEING YOU ALL HERE. AS YOU KNOW WE ARE GOING TO PUT ON THE CHRISTMAS PLAY..."

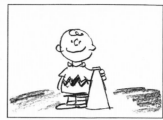

C.B: "DUE TO THE SHORTAGE OF TIME, WE'LL GET RIGHT DOWN TO WORK..."

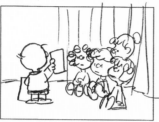

C.BROWN: "ONE OF THE FIRST THINGS TO INSURE A GOOD PERFORMANCE IS STRICT ATTENTION TO THE DIRECTOR."

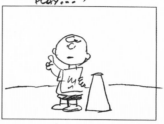

C.BROWN: "I'LL KEEP MY DIRECTIONS SIMPLE."

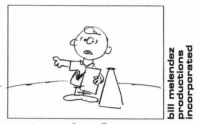

C.BROWN: "IF I POINT TO THE RIGHT — IT MEANS FOCUS ATTENTION TO STAGE RIGHT"

bill melendez productions incorporated

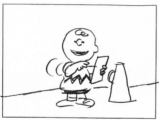

C.B. "IF I MAKE A SLASHING MOTION ACCROSS MY THROAT, IT MEANS CUT THE SCENE SHORT..."

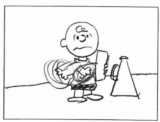

C.BROWN: "IF I MAKE A REVOLVING MOTION WITH MY HAND, IT MEANS, PICK UP THE TEMPO..."

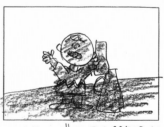

C.BROWN: "IF I SPREAD MY HANDS APART, IT MEANS SLOW DOWN,

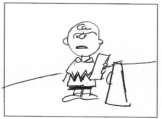

C.BROWN NOW VERY GLUM SEZ: "IT'S THE SPIRIT OF THE ACTORS THAT COUNTS, THE INTEREST THAT THEY SHOW, IN THEIR DIRECTOR."

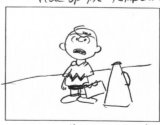

C.BROWN: "AM I RIGHT? I SAID, AM I RIGHT?"

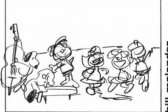

KIDS ARE DANCING WILDLY, THE JERK, FRUG, WATUSI, ETC

bill melendez productions incorporated

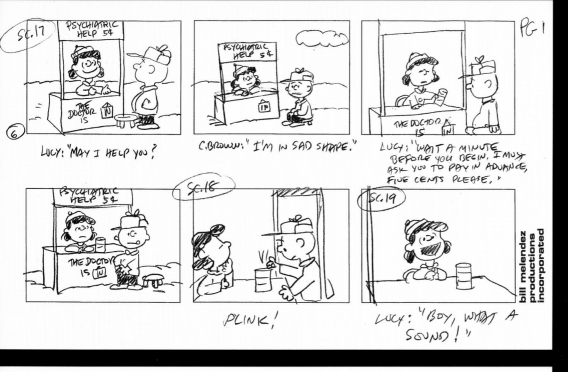

SC.17

6

LUCY: "MAY I HELP YOU?"

C.BROWN: "I'M IN SAD SHAPE."

LUCY: "WAIT A MINUTE BEFORE YOU BEGIN, I MUST ASK YOU TO PAY IN ADVANCE, FIVE CENTS PLEASE."

SC.18

SC.19

PLINK!

LUCY: "BOY, WHAT A SOUND!"

bill melendez
productions
incorporated

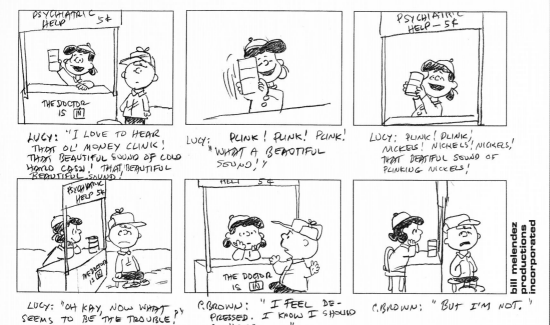

LUCY: "I LOVE TO HEAR THAT OL' MONEY CLINK! THAT BEAUTIFUL SOUND OF COLD HARD CASH! THAT BEAUTIFUL BEAUTIFUL SOUND!

LUCY: PLINK! PLINK! PLINK! "WHAT A BEAUTIFUL SOUND!"

LUCY: PLINK! PLINK! NICKELS! NICKELS! NICKELS! THAT BEATIFUL SOUND OF PLINKING NICKELS!

LUCY: "OH KAY, NOW WHAT SEEMS TO BE THE TROUBLE?"

C.BROWN: "I FEEL DE-PRESSED. I KNOW I SHOULD BE HAPPY...."

C.BROWN: "BUT I'M NOT."

bill melendez
productions
incorporated

PROD. No. 64-4   TITLE A Charlie Brown Christmas   FILM 2318'

Sc.	SCREEN FTG.	ANIM FTG.	ANIMATOR	ACTION	LAYOUT	BG's	STOCK ANIM.	ASST.	FINAL TEST	CHKG.	I-P.	PROD. CAMERA	CUT.
1	69²	16⁵	FRANK	LINUS & CHARLIE YAK ON WAY TO ICE POND	PAN	ED	X				v		
2	26²	30⁵	BOB E.	KIDS SKATE SNOOPY SPINS WHIP	PAN	ED	X	8-5-65	v		v	v	
3	10²			SNOOPY SNAPS UP CHARLIE & LINUS	SA-2	ED	X		v		v	v	
4	7⁸			CHARLIE INTO MAIN TITLE	PAN	ED	X		v			v	
5	11³	3	FRANK	SNOOPY TOSSES LINUS TO SIGN	SA-2	K	X		v		v	v	
6	8⁴	3		CHARLIE PUTS ON COAT	STILL	K	X		v		v	Ⓧ	
7	35⁴			CHARLIE GOES TO MAIL BOX	PAN	K	X		v		v	Ⓧ	
8	16⁵			CHARLIE SEES SNOOPY READING	STILL	K	X		v		v	Ⓧ	
9	48	1⁵	BOB C.	KIDS WATCH IT SNOW	STILL	K			v		v	v	
10	3⁰			C.S. LUCY CATCHING SNOW FLAKE	CARD	K			v		v	v	
11	6⁴	1⁵		P.S. LINUS	SA-10	K			v		v	v	
12	16⁵	5⁵	H	KID THRO SNOWBALLS AT CAN	SA-9	K	()		v		v	v	
13	14¹²	4⁵	V	LINUS HITS CAN	STILL	K			v			v	
13A	10¹²			LINUS GOES PAST KIDS	SA-9	K			v			v	
13E	13⁸		XENIA	CHARLIE GOES TO PSYCHIATRIC STAND	SA-15	E			v		v	v	
14	18	16	BOB C.	SCHROEDER TELLS LUCY	SA-9	K	X		v			v	
15	9²		FRANK	CHARLIE AT STAND WAITS LUCY	PAN	E	X		v			(v)	
16	3²			HELD SC.	STILL	E	X		v		v	v	
17	16⁵	5		LUCY RINGS INT. CAN & CHARGES	SA-15	E	X		v		v	v	
18	3¹²			CHARLIE PUTS COIN INTO CAN	STILL	E	X		v		v	v	
19	2⁴	0⁰⁵		C.S. LUCY SEZ:	SA-15	E	X		v			v	
20	7¹⁰	3⁵		M.S. LUCY & CHARLIE	SA-15	E	X		v			v	
21	17⁸	2		CHARLIE COMPLAINS TO LUCY	PAN	E	X		v			v	
22	10⁵	3		LUCY YAKS AT CHARLIE	SA-15	E	X		v			v	
23	8⁴			C.S. LUCY	SA-15	E	X		v			v	
24	7¹¹	1⁵		ECU LUCY	SA-10	E	X		v			v	
25+26	18⁵	2²		L.S. LUCY & CHARLIE	SA-21	E	X		v			(v)	
27	5⁴			C.S. LUCY SAYS:	SA-15	E	X		v			v	
28	18⁶	6⁵		L.S. LUCY & CHARLIE	SA-21	E	X		v		v	v	
29	7²			L.S. LUCY & CHARLIE	SA-15	E	X		v		v	v	
30	21⁰	8		M.S. LUCY & CHARLIE	SA-15	E	X		v		v	v	
31	7⁸			P.S. CHARLIE	SA-10	E	X		v		v	v	
32	6⁵	1⁵		C.S. LUCY	SA-15	E	X		v			v	
33	55²	15		M.S. LUCY & CHARLIE - FOLLOWS SNOOPY	SA-15	E	X		v		v	v	
35	21⁰	7	R. KOSTEN	L.S. SNOOPY DECORATES HOUSE	PAN	E	⊗		v		v	v	
35A	16⁵	1	XENIA	C.S. CHARLIE IS AGHAST	SA-10	K	X		v		v	v	
36	8⁴		XENIA	SNOOPY DECORATES HOUSE	STILL	K	X		v		v	v	
2A	4⁵		BILL	PAN OF KIDS FACES	SA-15	E	X		v		v	v	
11A	12		BARBARA	M.S. KIDS LOOK AT SNOW - LUCY SEZ:	SA-9	K	X		v		v	v	
11B	4⁸	4	BOB C.	P.S. LINUS SEZ	SA-10	K	X		v		v	v	
8A	25⁸	7	BOB C.	VIOLET BLAST CHARLIE	SA-1	K	X		v		v	v	
8B	48⁸	13		BIG PEN BLASTS CHARLIE	BILL	K	X		v		v	v	
13B	10	7	BOB C.	LUCY YELLS A LINUS	CARD	K	X		v			v	
13C	9²	2		LINUS YELLS AT LUCY	"	K	X		v			v	
13D	2¹			LUCY IS STRUCK DUMB	"	K	X		v			v	
13E	3¹²			CHARLIE WALKS AWAY	SA-9	K	X		v			v	
36A	29⁴	8	RUDY	SALLY ACCOSTS CHARLIE	PAN	E	X		v		v	v	
36B	7⁸			P.S. SALLY YAKS	CARD	E	X		v		v	v	
37	49⁸	12⁵		CHARLIE & SALLY	SA-36A	E	X		v		v	v	
38	21	6		L.S. KIDS DANCE	STILL	K			v		v	v	
39	8⁵		RUDY	C.S. LUCY YELLS AT KIDS	CARD	K			v			v	
40	14²	4		C.S. VIOLET LUCY & PATTY	STILL	K			v			v	
41	12	3		M.S. LUCY & KIDS WELCOME DIRECTION	SA-40	K			v			v	
41A	14¹			KIDS APPLAUD & BOO CHARLIE	SA-40	K			v			v	
42	12⁴	1⁵	ALAN	CHARLIE YAKS TO KIDS	PAN	B	X		v			v	
43	7¹⁴			SA-42	B	X			v			v	
44	34⁵	10		CHARLIE HEADS STRIPE	SA-42	B			v			v	
45				KIDS DANCE	SA-38	B							
46	18⁴	4⁵		C.S. CHARLIE YAKS	SA-42	B			v			v	
47	24⁴	4		LUCY GIVES SONJA & BIG PEN COSTUME	SA-42	B	X		v			v	
47B	13²			SHERMY GETS COSTUME	SA-42	B	X		v			v	
47C	58⁸	18		LUCY GIVES SNOOPY HIS SCRIPT	SA-42	B	X		v			v	
48	7¹⁴	1⁵	MANUEL	CHARLIE YELLS AT LUCY	SA-42	B	X		v		v	v	
49	22¹⁵		HERM	LUCY HANDS PART TO LINUS	STILL	B			v		v	v	
50	8⁸	3⁶		LINUS EXPLODES	SA-49	B			v		v	v	
51				LUCY & LINUS		B							
52	11⁶	4		LUCY THREATEN LINUS	SA-49	B			v			v	
53	7¹⁴	2		P.S. LINUS SEZ	CARD	B			v			v	
54	16²	9¹²	RUDY	LUCY YELLS AGAIN AT LINUS	SA-44	B			v			v	
55	9¹²		TIMMINS	LINUS TWIRLS BLANKET ABOUT HEAD	"	B			v			v	
56	15¹²	4	HERM	CHARLIE TELLS EM TO QUIET DOWN	SA-42		X		v			v	
56A	48		HERM	SCHROEDER PLAYS	SA-38		X		v			v	
B			HERM			B							
C	60⁵	17		SONJA & BIG PEN	SA-42	B			v			v	
D	31²			CHARLIE CALLS SALLY	SA-49	B			v			v	
E	4⁵	1		LINUS SEZ:	CARD	B			v			v	
F	2¹³			CHARLIE & LINUS	SA-49	B			v			v	
G	20¹²	6	RUDY	SALLY FALLS FOR LINUS	CARD	B			v			v	
H	2-8			LUCY YELLS WHICH ROENN	CARD	B			v			v	
J	28-0	8	RUDY	CHARLIE LISTENS	SA-56	B			v		v	v	
J	37⁴		RUDY	LUCY ARGUES WITH CHARLIE	SA-54	B			v		v	v	
K	20⁴	6	RUDY	LUCY CHARGES OUT	SA-54	B			v		v	v	
				(CHARLIE YELLS FOR QUIET AGAIN)		B							
57	10⁵			KIDS DANCE	SA-38	B			v				
58	10⁵	3	RUDY	CHARLIE GRABS MEGAPHONE	SA-54	B			v			v	
59	11⁵	4	LITTLE FINN	CHARLIE STOPS DANCE	SA-8	B			v			v	
60	24²		RUDY	LUCY ASKS CHARLIE WHAT'S UP	SA-42	B	X		v			v	
61A	15⁴	4		GET A TREE LUCY SEZ	SA-42	B			v			v	
62	28-0	9		LUCY TALKS CHARLIE INTO ACTION	SA-42	B	X		v			v	
64	18²	4⁶	MARTIN	CHARLIE & LINUS LEAVE AUDITORIUM	PAN				v				
66	48	1	M	L.S. BENCH KIDS	STILL	E	X		v			v	
67	48	1	M	C.S. KIDS - LINUS SEZ:	SA-10	E	X		v			v	
67A	5⁰		M	KIDS WALK ON	SA-66	E	X		v			v	
68	6⁵	1	M	KID IN LOT	STILL	E			v			v	
69	7⁵	2	M	KIDS LOOK AT TREES	STILL	E	X		v			v	
70	25⁸			XMAS TREE LOT	STILL	E			v			v	
71	54		M	LINUS & CHARLIE BY TREE	SA-70	B			v			v	
72	24⁴	8	BILL FINN	CHARLIE TREES TREE	STILL	B	X		v			v	
73	167⁴	48		SCHROEDER PLAYS PIANO	STILL				v				

PROD. No. 64-4   TITLE A CHARLIE BROWN CHRISTMAS   FILM

Sc.	SCREEN FTG.	ANIM FTG.	ANIMATOR	ACTION	LAYOUT	BG's.	ANIM.	ASST.	FINAL TEST	CHKG.	I-P.	PROD. CAMERA	CUT.
74	11⁹	4	RUDI	CHARLIE & LINUS RETURN	SA-84						✓		
75	4⁵		↓	C.S. CHARLIE LINUS & SHROEDER							✓		
76	6⁸	3	RUSS	KIDS GATHER AROUND TREE							✓		
77	15⁴	4	FRANK	VIOLET WCY & PATTY RIP INTO CHARLIE	CARD + SA 42						✓		
78	9⁰		↓	VIOLET PIG PEN & SALLY (VIOLET SE2)							✓		
79	6³	2	RUDI	PATTY JUMPS CHARLIE TOO	SD 42						✓		
80	2⁹	1	RUSS	CATANLY SES: RATS							✓		
81	8⁸	2	↓	CHARLIE & TREE	SA 76						✓		
82	12⁹			SNOOPY LAFS HYSTERICALLY							✓		
83	6⁸		RUBIN FRANK S.	L.S. SHROEDER & KIDS WALK AT	↓						◯		
84											◯		
85	32²	7	ROSEN	LINUS ONTO STAGE	STILL	E					◯		
86	63⁰	18	↓	LINUS TELLS STORY	STILL	E							
87	21⁵			CHARLIE WATCHES LINUS EXIT	SA 84								
88	17⁰	3⁷⁸	RUSS V.N.	CHARLIE EXITS	PAN	E			✓		✓		
89	22·10		↓	CHARLIE OUT IN FIELD (89A·89B)	PAN	E			✓		✓		
89C				CHARLIE ONTO STARS	STILL				✓				
90	27⁶	6			↓				✓				
91									✓				
92	13¹³	3		L.S. CHARLIE WALKS	SA-89				✓		✓		
93	12	6	JOHN WALK	CHARLIE ON WAY HOME	PAN				✓		✓		
94	4¹		RUBIN	CHARLIE AT DOG HOUSE	PAN				✓		✓		
94A	4⁴	1	↓		STILL				✓		✓		
95	3	—	MANUEL	CHARLIE LOOKING	STILL	×			✓		✓		
96	42¹⁰	14	MANUEL	CHARLIE KILLS TREE	SA 94				✓				
99	16⁵	50	RUDI	LINUS BLANKETS TREE	STILL						✓		
100	9·7	3	JOHN WALK	KIDS DECORATE TREE	SA-94						✓		
101	11·10	3	↓	KIDS' REVEAL TREE	SA 99						✓		
103		12	HELM								✓		
109	77⁴	20	RUBIN	END TITLES 16 F	STILL	E							
SCA				MUSIC INTRO PAN TO SKATING	SA 2								
				PAN FROM HOUSE	SA-64								
				WALK TO DISTANCE	SA-66								
					SD-66A								
				WALK TO WALL	SA-1 / SA 35								

The complete, original scene production sheets for production number 64-4, *A Charlie Brown Christmas*.

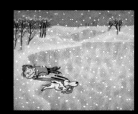

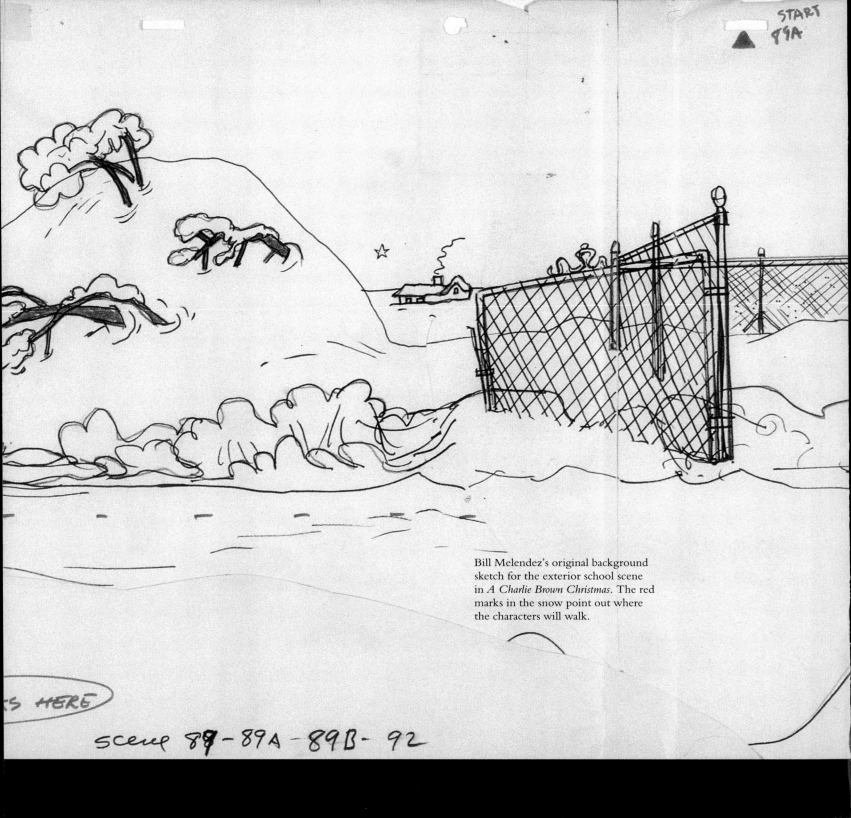

Bill Melendez's original background
sketch for the exterior school scene
in *A Charlie Brown Christmas*. The red
marks in the snow point out where
the characters will walk.

S HERE

scene 89 - 89A - 89B - 92

START POS. 89

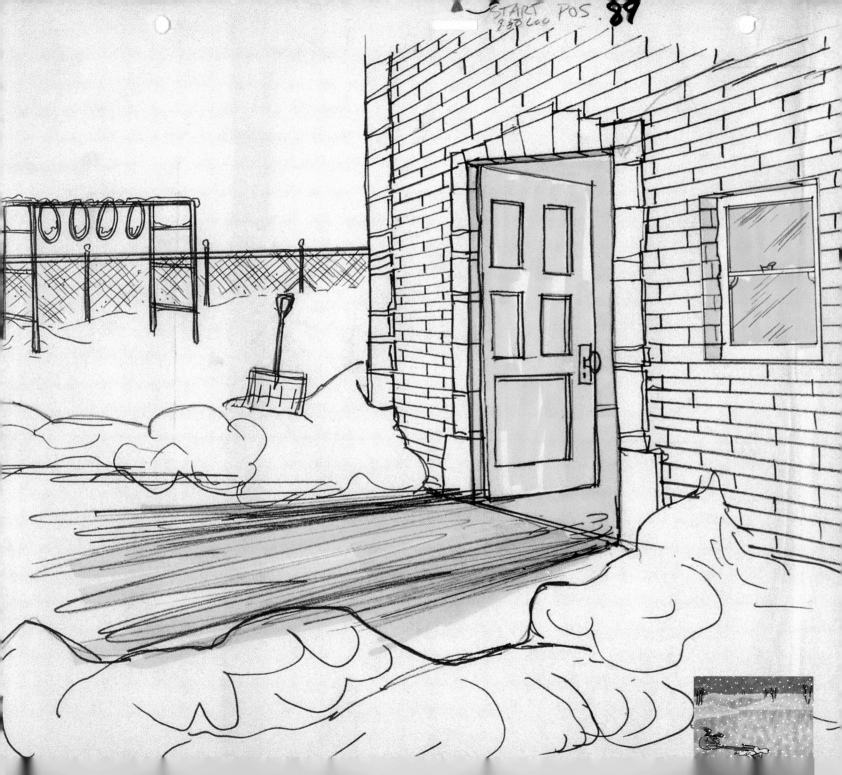

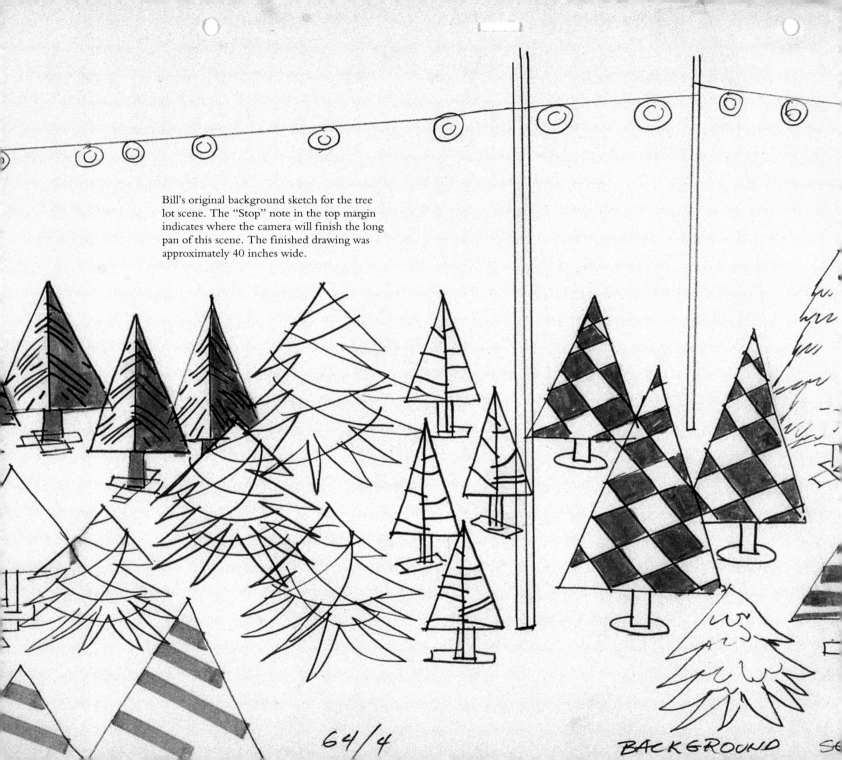

Bill's original background sketch for the tree lot scene. The "Stop" note in the top margin indicates where the camera will finish the long pan of this scene. The finished drawing was approximately 40 inches wide.

64/4

BACKGROUND

1 STOP
TREE ON CELL
NE 70-71

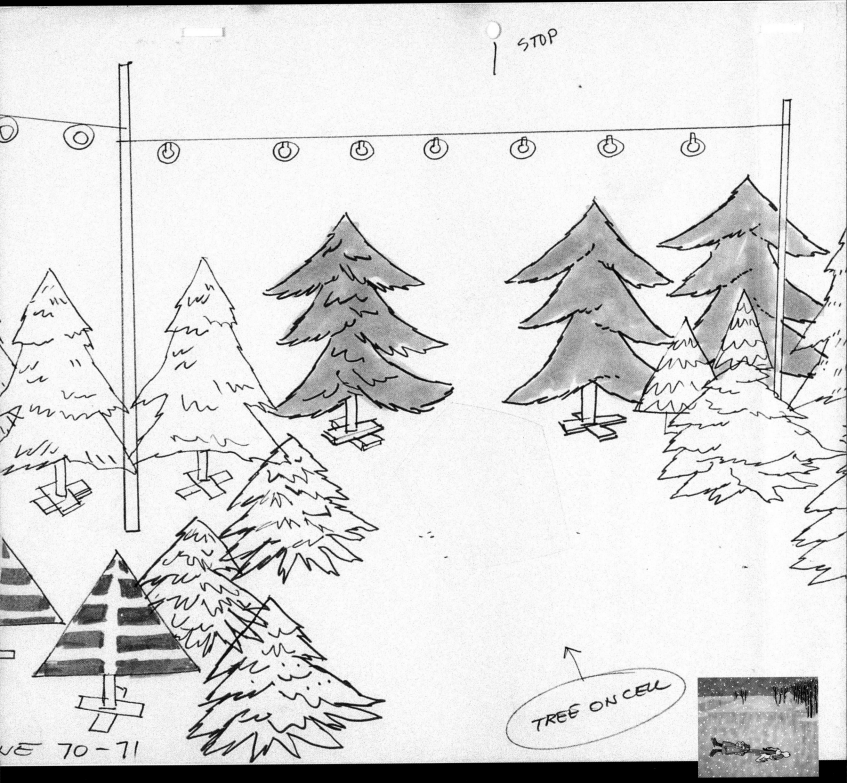

NOTE: 1ˢᵀ COMMERCIAL IS AT 141³',
      2ᴰ " " " 1648⁰·

PG-1

Sc. 1 _ 62⁹

PROD 64-4 "A CHARLIE BROWN CHRISTMAS"

X DISS FROM SC. A
ROCK WALL - IT'S
SNOWING GENTLY

CHARLIE
BROWN
FOLLOWED
BY
LINUS ENTERS — THEY WALK IN BEHIND WALL

24 X DISS FROM INTRO

| | 3X | 10X | 2X | 6X | 6X | 1X | 5X | 6X | 2X |

ST ST ST ST ST

TEMPO - 13X
METRONOME 110

13X   13X   13X   3·⁴

CONT

CHARLIE
TURNS TO
WALL

LEANS ON
WALL
SADLY

| 4X | 6X | 3X | 3X | 6X | 4X | 2X | 6X | 5X | 1X | 6X | 6X |

ST ST ST ST ST ST ST ST

13X   13X.   13X   13X   6·⁵

LINUS
LOOKS
AT
CHARLIE (CONT WALKING)

LINUS
STOPS
LOOKS
AT CHARLY (HOLD SCENE)

| 6X | 6X | 1X | 5X | 8X |

ST

13X   13X   13X   13X   9·¹²

bill melendez
productions
incorporated

⑦
LINUS
STICKS
THUMB
IN
MOUTH & STEPS UP TO
WALL
ST ST
* *
6X

LEANS
ON
WALL
LOOKING
AT CHARLIE
7X

⑧
CHARLIE
TURNS TO
LINUS
SAYING:

I THINK THERE MUST BE

LO LO LO

→ PIANO SNOW BALL MUSIC

13Y   13X   11⁶   13X   13X   13⁰

⑨   ⑩

SOMETHING WRONG WITH ME LINUS ———— CHRISTMAS IS CO—

13X   13X   13 X   13X   16⁴

⑪   ⑫

TURNS
GLUMLY
BACK TO
STARING
TO SPACE

MING —— BUT I'M NOT HAPPY ————
11Y   2X   6X   1   7X

13X   13X   13X   13X   19⁸

⑬　⑭

DON'T FEEL THE WAY I'M SUPPOSED TO FEEL

1x　12x

13x　13x　13x　13x　22¹²⁄

⑮ ⑯

CHARLIE LINUS
PULLS ALSO AND THEY WALK ON
BACK

PAN B.G. LEFT

ST　ST　ST　ST　ST　ST　ST

1x　5x　6x　2x　4x　6x　3x　3v　6x　4x

13x　13x　13x　13x　26⁰

⑰ ⑱

CHARLIE
SEZ:

DON'T PAN

ST　ST　ST　ST　ST　ST　ST　ST

2x　6x　5x　1x　6y　6x　6x　6v　1x　5x　6x　2x

I JUST DON'T UNDERSTAND

13x　13x　13x　13x　29⁴⁄

bill melendez
productions
incorporated

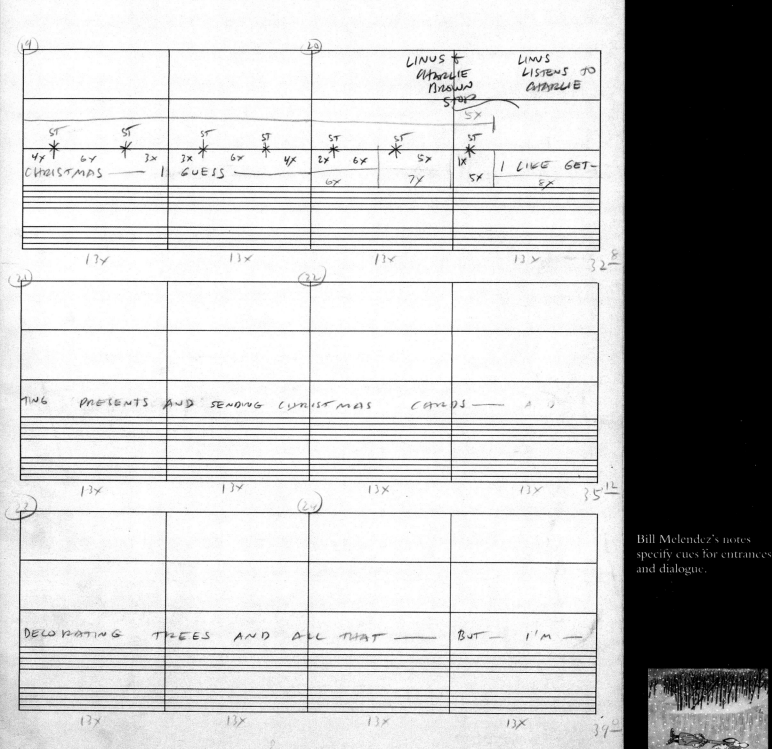

PG-4

Bill Melendez's notes specify cues for entrances and dialogue.

PG 5

PROD 64-4

25 26

LINUS
TURNS ← WALKS ON
AS CHARLIE
FOLLOWS &
SEZ:

PAN

STILL   NOT   HAPPY

ST   ST
5x   3x   2x 5x   1 1x
3x   5x

13x   13x   13x   13x   42⁴

27 28

CONT PAN   STOP
                                             PAN

ST   ST   ST   ST   ST   ST   ST   ST
5x   6x 2x 4x   6x   3x 3x   6x   4x   2x   6x   5x
ALWAYS   END   UP   FEELING   DEPRESSED
                                             6x   7x

13x   13x   13x   13x   45⁵

29 30

LINUS ZELAS   SEZ:
HE TURNS
                   CHARLIE
                   BROWN
ST
CHARLIE   BROWN   CHARLIE BROWN   —   YOU'RE   THE   ONLY   —

13x   13x   13x   13x   48¹²

bill melendez
productions
incorporated

PG 6

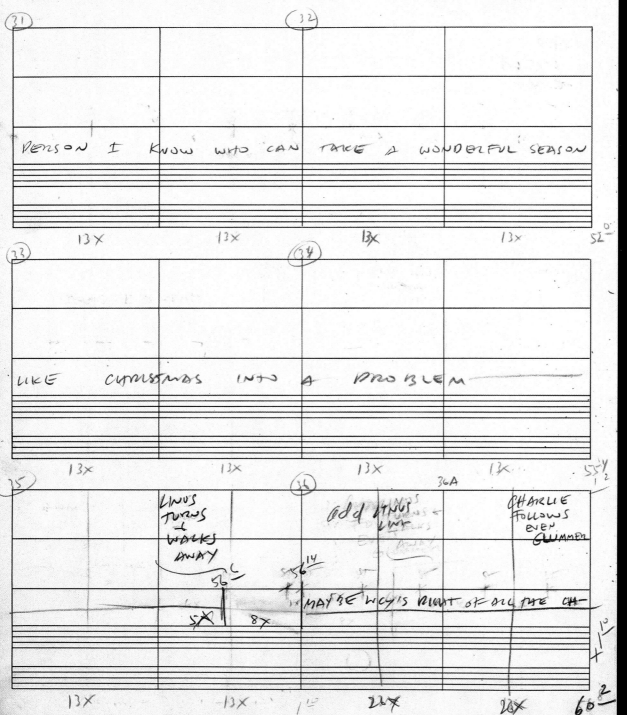

PERSON I KNOW WHO CAN TAKE A WONDERFUL SEASON

13X   13X   13X   13X   52⁰

LIKE CHRISTMAS INTO A PROBLEM

13X   13X   13X   13X   55 ¼

LINUS TURNS + WALKS AWAY

odd LINUS LINE

CHARLIE FOLLOWS EVEN GLIMMER

MAYBE LUCY'S RIGHT OF ALL THE CH—

13X   13X   22X   20X   60²

When the bar sheets were ready, composer Vince Guaraldi wrote music that fit into specific time frames from scene to scene.

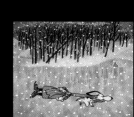

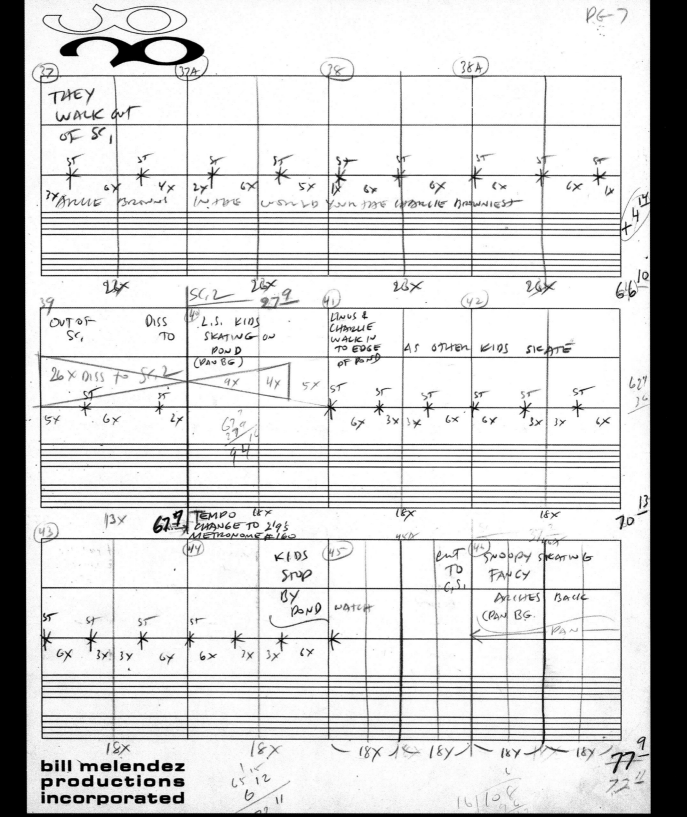

bill melendez
productions
incorporated

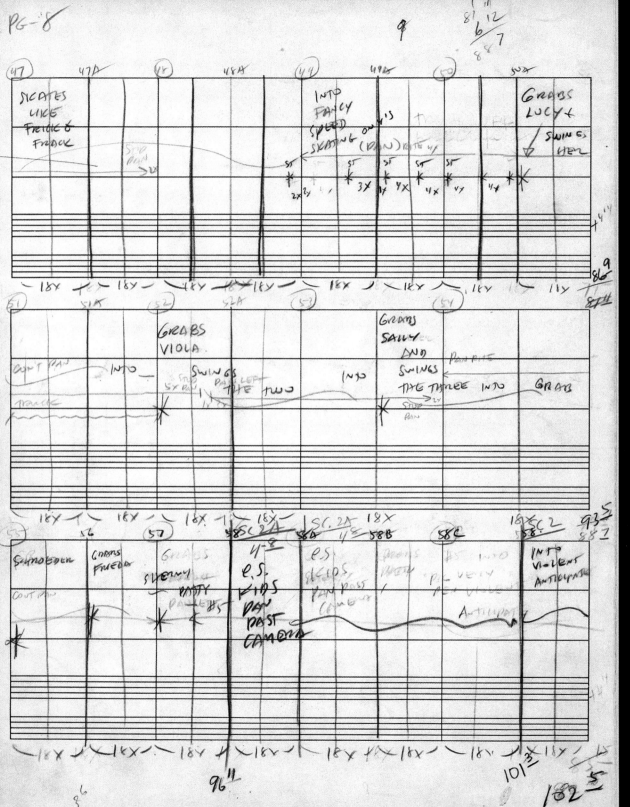

Many layers of information describe part of the opening skating sequence.

Ɔ∞ PROD 64-4

59	60		61			62	
	CRACK!		SNOOPY		PAN	SNOOPY	PAN
	LINE		SPINS	TO LEFT	SLOWS	STOPS	STOPS
STOP PAN	SHOOTS OFF		PAN			ON BELLY AS—	
	IN ALL DIRECTIONS					LINUS ENTERS	2X AS—
				4 8		CHARLIE FOLLOWS	
			24				
18X	18X		18X		18X		13
							106

63		64		SC. 3 10	65		66	
LINUS AND			LINUS HAS		ZONK!		
CHARLIE			THUMB IN		SNOOPY HITS		
BROWN SKATING — PAN WITH LINUS			MOUTH BLANKET BY EAR		BLANKET — ROLLS LINUS PAN SPEEDS UP		
STOP PAN			PAN				
3X							
18X		9X 108		18X		18X		14
							141

67		68		69		70	
SNOOPY TURNS CORNER		ZONK!			SLIDES TO STOP		
		PICKS UP CHARLIE					
		BROWN — PULL HIM ALONG					
STOP PAN		PAN WITH DOG					
18X	18X		18X		18X		

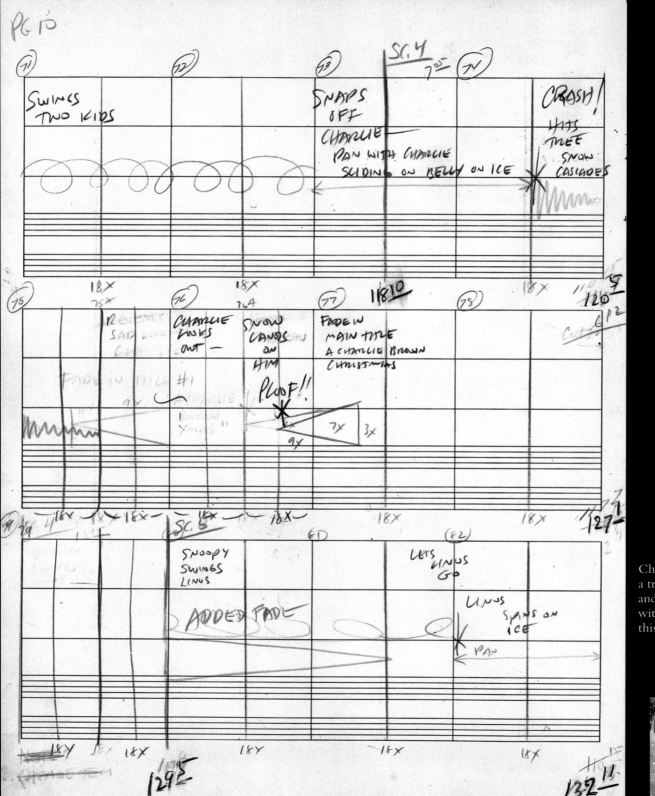

PG 10

SC. 4
7⁰⁵

SWINGS TWO KIDS

SNAPS OFF CHARLIE — PAN WITH CHARLIE SLIDING ON BELLY ON ICE

CRASH! HITS TREE SNOW CASCADES

18X   18X   11810   18X   120

CHARLIE LOOKS OUT —   SNOW LANDS ON HIM   FADE IN MAIN TITLE A CHARLIE BROWN CHRISTMAS

PLOOF!!   9X   7X   3X

SC. 5   127

SNOOPY SWINGS LINUS

LETS LINUS GO

ADDED FADE

LINUS SPINS ON ICE   PAN

18X   18X   18X   18X   18X   18X   18X

1295   1322

Charlie Brown slides into a tree with a "CRASH!" and snow covers him with a "PLOOF!" in this sequence.

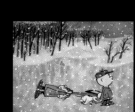

GRETSCH

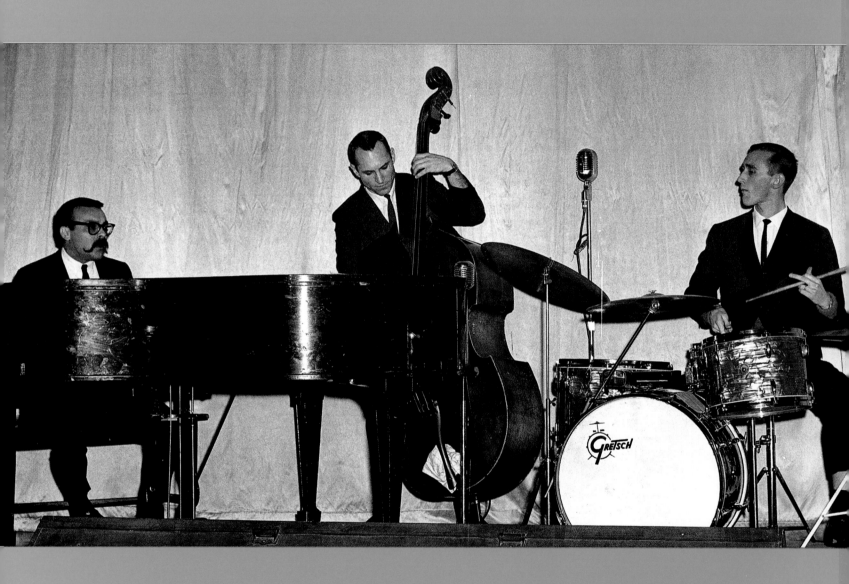

vince guaraldi, composer

the music of Vince Guaraldi has been a vital part of the *Peanuts* television specials since the first broadcast of *A Charlie Brown Christmas,* in 1965. Two years before, the San Francisco–based jazz pianist had won a Grammy for "Cast Your Fate to the Wind," an instrumental recorded with his trio. The record, featuring Guaraldi with drummer Colin Bailey and bassist Monty Budwig, went gold and was the first hit for Fantasy Records.

When Lee Mendelson was working on his documentary about Schulz in 1963 and heard "Cast Your Fate to the Wind" in his car, he was mesmerized. "It was a sound like I'd never heard before," he said. "It was jazz, but it was melodic and open and came like a breeze off the bay." He immediately commissioned Guaraldi to write music for the documentary, and although the show didn't get sold to a network, Fantasy Records released Guaraldi's sound track, *Jazz Impressions of "A Boy Named Charlie Brown."* When Mendelson set out to produce *A Charlie Brown Christmas* in 1965, Guaraldi was brought in to rework some of the themes from the doc–umentary and create a new sound track for the television special. *A Charlie Brown Christmas* went platinum (sold 1 million copies) in 1997, and remains one of the top-selling holiday albums every year.

Vince Guaraldi called himself a "reformed boogie-woogie piano player," and made his start playing in a variety of trios and bands in the San Francisco Bay area. He went on the road for a couple of years in the 1950s with Woody Herman's big band, but did most of his play–ing in colleges and the beatnik clubs of San Francisco. Nicknamed "Dr. Funk" by his jazz friends, Guaraldi was an exotic figure on the local scene with his trademark mustache and ever-changing hairstyles.

LEFT: The Vince Guaraldi Trio in 1962, with Vince Guaraldi on piano, Monty Budwig on bass, and Colin Bailey on drums.

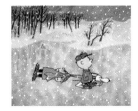

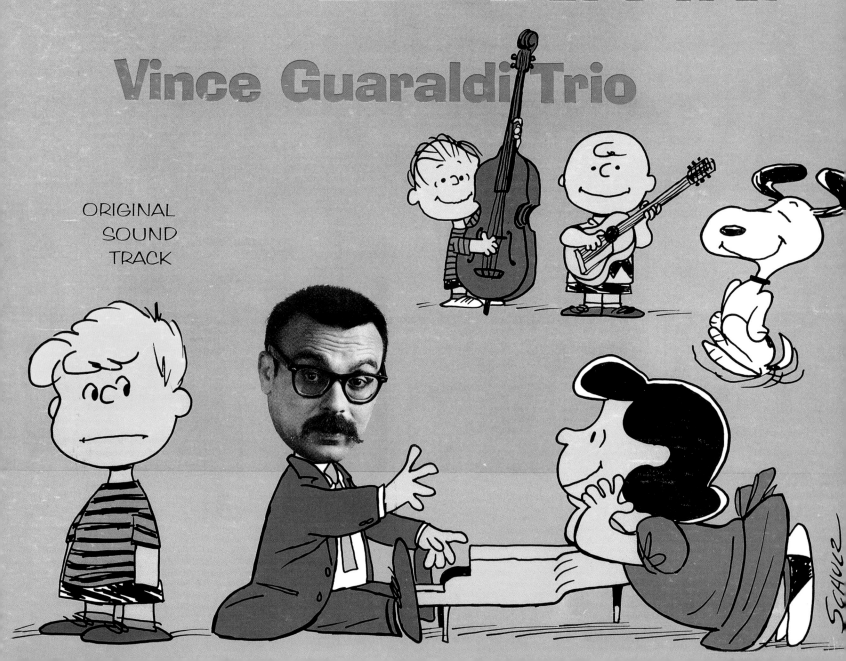

STEREO
85017

STEREO

MONAURAL
5017

JAZZ IMPRESSIONS of "A BOY NAMED

Fantasy Records
HIGH FIDELITY

CHARLIE BROWN"

Vince Guaraldi Trio

ORIGINAL
SOUND
TRACK

"Vince was perfect for all of us," recalled Bill Melendez. "He was easy to work with, like Schulz. When I finished the storyboards for *A Charlie Brown Christmas* and showed him my bar sheets, the pages that show the music and dialogue cues for each scene, he'd say, 'Just tell me how many yards you want.' By yards he meant seconds of music."

"Vince had won the Grammy and toured all over the country," said Lee Mendelson, "but once he started Charlie Brown, it practically became his whole life. He stayed mostly in San Francisco. He worked on the shows and became totally absorbed with it, doing the first 15 shows for us. He was very contemporary and very improvisational, which gave *A Charlie Brown Christmas* and the other shows a hip sound. Vince was a high-energy guy with a great sense of humor, and our meetings were very stimulating. I used to have to pat him on the head sometimes and just say, 'Relax.' He was always writing and never had a problem with deadlines. If I called him up one day and

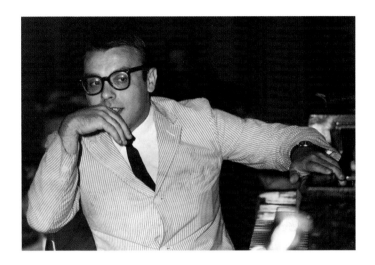

LEFT: Guaraldi's first *Peanuts* album was written as a sound track for the 1963 documentary about Charles Schulz, *A Boy Named Charlie Brown*. Two years later, several pieces from this album, including "Linus and Lucy," were included on the sound track for *A Charlie Brown Christmas*.

"He was very contemporary and very improvisational, which gave A Charlie Brown Christmas *and the other shows a hip sound."*

—Lee Mendelson

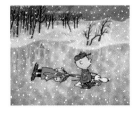

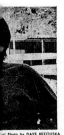

Photo by DAVE BEZOUSKA

of the jazz hit "Cast
and 10 p.m. tonight
The Lockheed Bag-
appeared in concert
rrently working on
ies, "Yours in Love,
formances is $1.75

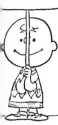

A
"A
CHARLIE
BROWN
CHRISTMAS"

U. S. Pat. Off.—All rights reserved
by United Feature Syndicate, Inc.

hit—and he

thoven wasn't so great.
you ever seen his picture
ubble gum cards?" At
r point, asked what she
wants for Christmas,
nswers: "Real estate,"
nother time she notes
's well known that
s is commercial, and
run by a big Eastern

to say, Charlie
lly gets his message
ut as might be
hat crazy-silly-won-
Snoopy was the
every time he
laying the gui-
er, His doghouse,
, was wildly
all those ugly
sing des'gns that
also have been
their homes at

words should
pianist *Vince*
gentle, mood-
ich—uniquely
half-hour en-
ractive con-
ature in an
ticing way,

Experiment in Jazz--With the Under 14

By Jon Carroll

IN A BARE rehearsal hall, decorated only with large, black on yellow "No Smoking" signs, the Vince Guaraldi Trio practices for a concert. They're playing the standard numbers from their act — "Yesterday" by Paul McCartney, "Blowin' in the Wind" by a young man named Dylan, and, of course, "Cast Your Fate To The Winds," their Hit.

In itself, it is an unremarkable scene. Standing behind the trio, however, are 60 members of the San Francisco Boys Chorus. As the trio plays, and Guaraldi does his little baroque bits on the piano, the boys carry the melody with their clear soprano voices.

Jazz with an all-boy soprano chorus? You betcha.

Guaraldi has always liked to work with kids. Last year, he worked with a children's chorus for his Mass for Grace Cathedral. He did the score for the animated cartoons of the comic strip "Peanuts," and next year plans to record 'The Charlie Brown Suite,' based on his music for the cartoons, with a full symphony orchestra.

In his spare time, Guaraldi has worked for the Title III program, a Federal government project which brings music to underprivileged youngsters. Last year he took his trio to Merced County.

The Magnificent Moustache

"I dig working with kids," said Guaraldi after the rehearsal, his magnificent moustache moving as he spoke. (Someday a story will be written about Vince Guaraldi without mentioning his

VINCE GUARALDI

moustache. This is not it). "They have a sound — a timbre — that's really better than adults doing the same stuff. It's the simplicity that counts. No . . . no filigree."

The Boys Chorus is a remarkable group to work with. Formed 19 years ago as an adjunct to the San Francisco Opera, the 100 boys involved (drawn, as they say, from all races and creeds) go through rigorous training in the five or so years they

Ralph Gleason is on vacation. His column will be resumed upon his return.

are members. From the youngest (usually 8 years old) to the oldest (until his voice changes — he's usually washed up at 14), they practice twice a week, give concerts, perform in operas, and attend a month-long summer camp which combines classes in singing and music theory with more traditional recreation.

After the Guaraldi rehearsal, for instance, a few boys stayed behind to practice

for auditions for Mozart's "The Magic Flute." And next week, a number of boys are performing in "Carmen" with the Opera Company.

Current leader of the chorus is young, graying Donald Cobb, a classical composer (one of his works will be done at the Cabrillo Music Festival) and teacher at Holy Names College.

What all these people — men and boys — are doing in that bare rehearsal hall is practicing for today's jazz concert at Stern Grove, the second jazz show ever held in that classical bastion. Last year's show — which also featured Guaraldi — attracted 25,000 people, with more turned away, who jammed the Grove for the four-hour concert. "They were hanging from the trees. I mean, they were hanging from the TREES," said Guaraldi.

At the close of the rehearsal, the principals retired to the inevitable metal folding chairs in a corner of the hall and there, relaxing, talked about the problems inherent in the production. Cobb was cheerfully anxious about everything; Guaraldi, the professional, very cool.

Part of the Charm

One problem was that they had to use more boys than usual. In concert dates, only about 40, drawn from the very top in experience and ability, perform. But, said Cobb, "Vince wanted more strength, so we're using some other boys. Some of the little ones in the front row are only eight, and this is their first concert. They're not doing everything quite right yet. And some of the kids in the second row have never sung parts before, and

I can hear them drift up to the melody."

"Yeah," said Guaraldi, "but that's part of the charm."

They were also planning to record the concert, and that worried Cobb too. "What happens if we make a mistake, if we do something wrong?" he asked Guaraldi.

"Then we get a tape with something wrong on it."

The results of this rehearsal — the experiment, really, in jazz, — will be on view today at 2 p.m. in Stern Grove. Also on the bill are Turk Murphy's Jazz Band, the folk-rock The Only Alternative and his Other Possibilities, and John Coppola and the Friends of Be Bop.

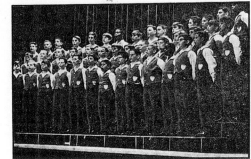

THE SAN FRANCISCO BOYS CHORUS

This World, Sunday, July 23, 1967

"Guaraldi is one of those jazz types who, after one concert, makes one sorry he ever jures up the thought of noise, makes one sorry he ever thought of the word."

— *The Evening Star, Wash. D.C.*

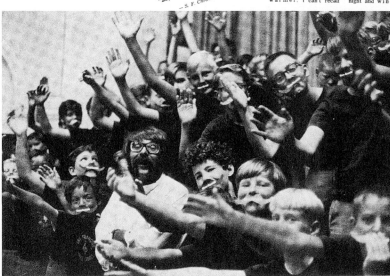

The Philadelphia Inquirer
Philadelphia, Pa. June 6, 1966

Screening TV

Baseball Manager Charlie Brown Almost Becomes Hero

By HARRY HARRIS
Of The Inquirer Staff

On the basis of Wednesday's "Charlie Brown's All-Stars" and its Yuletide predecessor, CBS' "Peanuts," specials aren't animated comic strips. They're animated tragic strips.

The new one, even better than the earlier prize-winner, told a sad little story about how baseball manager Charlie Brown almost became a hero after his team's 1000th lopsided loss. Almost.

Snoopy, as agile on the basepaths as on surfboard and skateboard (what a versatile pooch!) converted a single into a run by stealing second, third and home.

Charlie, who represented the typing run in the bottom of the ninth, tried to do the same.

Hesitating on third base, "It's hero time!" he shouted, "Geronimo!" style. "Here I go." "Here I stay." But finally he went.

"Slide, Charlie Brown, slide!" his appalled teammates caroled. He did. And was out by 30 feet!

So everyone yelled, "You blockhead, Charlie Brown!" and left him in despair, as they had done earlier when the new season began with a 123-0 defeat.

What made it seem even worse this time was that by not winning "one in a row" they apparently had lost Hennessey Hardward-emblazoned uniforms and a chance to play in a real league.

What Lucy, Freda, Snoopy and the others didn't know was that Charlie had turned down the uniforms

BEFORE the game because the league banned girls and dogs.

Linus knew, and told them, and then they were all sorry. Even Luch. And to prove it, they made Charlie an "Our Manager" uniform—out of Lachrymose Linus' blanket.

Next day Charlie, raring to go, was out there on the pitching mound—all alone in a teeming rain.

This bitter-sweet little yarn, written by "Peanuts" concocter, Charles M. Schulz, with original score by Vince Guaraldi and complete endearing pen-ink and-sound characterizations, was a lull-less delight.

San Francisco Examiner

Vince Guaraldi's Absence Makes the Hands Warmer

BY PHILIP ELWOOD

Absence, in the case of Vince Guaraldi, has made the heart and hands much warmer; I can't recall

"20,000 jam park for Vince Guaraldi"
— *S. F. Chronicle*

Vince in a more romantic or rhapsodic mood than he was last night in a long set at the Trident.

Perhaps the blustery night and wind-lashed

waves set the scene, certainly the Trident i cozy harbor in any sto But Guaraldi's refresh long flowing lines dem strated he hasn't been active during his long sence from the local cert and club routine.

"We've worked Ass twice since the New Y and played Boston. Ag a wild place during th season; I even got h on skiing." (Vince Gu di on skis?)

'A WORK YEAR'

"But nowhere in country has the kind of tistic action we h around San Francisco, even New York," he s "I'm glad to be home fo while; it looks like a w year."

Guaraldi's extended provisations on "Goin' C of My Head" and a ge geous original theme calls "Swan Song Blu were among the show best. And "It Was a Ve Good Year" and "Eleanc Rigby" had piano s quences of a type Guaral has never presented such thorough extensions.

COMFORTING

Gone as a dominant a pect of Guaraldi's treat ments is the full-blown La in beat. Retained is th light shifting bossa-nov shuffle — such hits a worked such hits a "Cast Your Fate to the Win."

It is remarkably beaut ful and comforting musi Drummer Jon Rae, wit his usual competence an musicianly approach, co tributes markedly to the fect. Bassist Kelly Bryan often hesitant and dul toned, but a few week with Guaraldi should war him up. He's a good techn cian.

"I was both honored and awe-struck at the tremendous beauty and sensitivity of your work"

— *Bishop James A. Pike*

"Pianist Vince Guaraldi's 'Cast Your Fate to the Wind' broke Fantasy Records' perfect record of 13½ solid years without a hit"

— *Herb Caen*

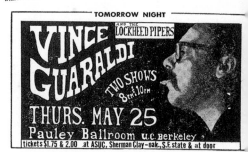
84

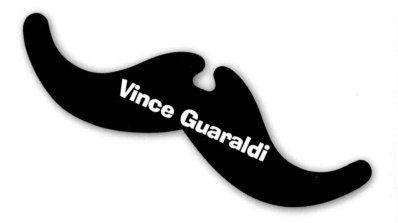

asked for a piece, he'd bring something over the next day."

"When *A Charlie Brown Christmas* was shown for the first time on television," said Vince Guaraldi's son, David, "it was a big event in my household and with my friends because it was the first *Peanuts* special. My dad was very excited. I was ten years old. My grandmother and great-grandmother came over to watch the show with us. *A Charlie Brown Christmas* was a hit right off the bat, and they did many more holiday specials after that. The music he wrote for the show relates to each scene and the *Peanuts* kids' feelings. He captured that perfectly because he loved kids; he did a lot of things for kids in his life. There was a lot of talk at school after the show and

LEFT: A collage of articles includes a story about Guaraldi rehearsing with the San Francisco Boys Chorus, for whom he had written arrangements of popular songs to be accompanied by his jazz trio in a 1967 concert. The previous year he performed with this chorus in his highly acclaimed Jazz Mass at San Francisco's Grace Cathedral. The boys in the photo are sporting black paper mustaches imprinted with Guaraldi's name, which were the jazz pianist/composer's trademark promotional pieces (right).

"He was a perfectionist

about everything he did,

and he was very serious

about his Peanuts *music."*

—David Guaraldi

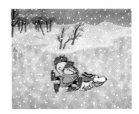

"A CHARLIE BROWN CHRISTMAS"

featuring the famous **PEANUTS** characters

ORIGINAL SOUND TRACK **Vince Guaraldi**

Fantasy Records ®

HIGH FIDELITY

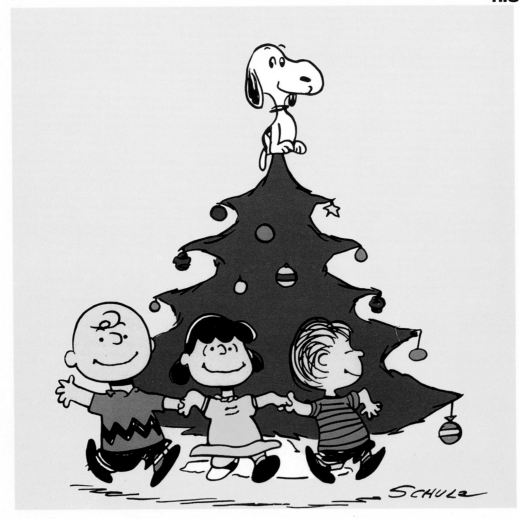

MONAURAL
5019

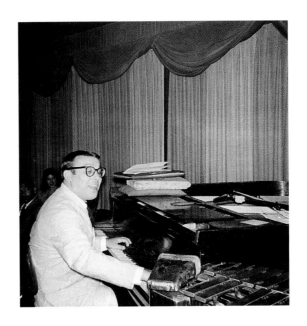

teachers and kids would come up to me to tell me how much they liked it. I'd get embarrassed over all the attention because I was so young, but I was very proud of my dad.

"He had a nine-foot grand piano in the living room and usually did his writing while my sister and I were at school. Sometimes I'd come home and he'd still be playing until dinnertime. When I was a teenager I'd help him carry his equipment to his jobs and stay up late waiting for him to finish. I'd fall asleep in the van until his gig was over and then help him break down his equipment and pack up. It was hard work, but it was fun.

"My dad was engulfed in the *Peanuts* music for many years," David Guaraldi continued. "That was his whole life. I don't understand how he found time to record his other albums and play locally at so many clubs. When he was working on a *Peanuts* show, he would drive down to L.A. to work with Bill Melendez and record at a studio at least twice a week. He was a perfectionist about everything he did, and he was very serious about his *Peanuts* music.

LEFT: Vince Guaraldi's sound track album to *A Charlie Brown Christmas* went platinum (sold over 1 million copies) and is one of the most popular holiday albums of all time.

"Guaraldi was one of the handful of pianists, like Dave Brubeck and Andre Previn, who made jazz piano popular, who crossed that bridge."

—*David Benoit*

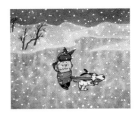

"The *Peanuts* music is very positive, just like all my dad's work. His personality was upbeat. When he performed he was really heavy into playing and he hummed out loud, pounding on the keyboard with his short fingers. Even his ballads and slower music or his heavy jazz music is positive. There's no downer about any of it. He was loved by a lot of jazz musicians he played with and by jazz pianists who played his music. After the Grammy and the many years of *Peanuts* shows, he became famous, but I don't think he realized it. The word famous never came up in our lives. "Linus and Lucy" is a big standard in this country, and it's a special thing to create something that lasts like that. Hearing my dad's music on the radio and the television always felt good. It's always going to feel good. I'm going to be eighty years old and still get goose bumps when I hear that music.

"My son is now ten years old and he watches the *Peanuts* cartoons on Nickelodeon every day," said David. "He knows who Papa Vince was and recognizes his music."

On February 6, 1976, just a few hours after finishing the sound track to his 15th *Peanuts* special, Vince Guaraldi died of a heart attack. Only 47 years old, he left behind a unique legacy in American jazz.

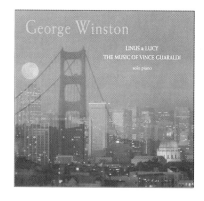

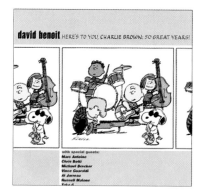

ABOVE RIGHT: Jazz pianists who have paid tribute to Vince Guaraldi include George Winston, who released *Linus and Lucy: The Music of Vince Guaraldi in 1996*. This album contains "Linus and Lucy," Guaraldi's most famous piece from *A Charlie Brown Christmas*. The most recent Guaraldi tribute album was released by jazz pianist David Benoit in May 2000. *Here's to You, Charlie Brown: 50 Great Years!* features Benoit's arrangements of pieces from *A Charlie Brown Christmas* and other specials.

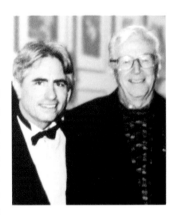

Jazz musicians who have created scores for the *Peanuts* animated shows since Vince Guaraldi's death include Dave Brubeck, George Winston, Wynton Marsalis, and David Benoit. Pianist George Winston, who has described Guaraldi as a major influence on his music, recorded an album tribute to his mentor in 1996 entitled *Linus and Lucy: The Music of Vince Guaraldi.* Another jazz pianist who credits Guaraldi as an important influence is David Benoit, who composed several *Peanuts* scores between 1988 and 2000. In May 2000, he released a tribute album entitled *Here's to You, Charlie Brown: 50 Great Years!,* which debuted at #2 on the *Billboard* jazz chart. This album contains two pieces from Guaraldi's *A Charlie Brown Christmas* sound track: Benoit's own version of "Linus and Lucy" (which opens with a few seconds of Guaraldi's original recording of the song) and a unique arrangement of "Christmas Time Is Here" with the vocal group Take 6.

Benoit wrote his first *Peanuts* score for *The Great Inventors,* one episode from the eight-part series *This Is America, Charlie Brown.* It was his first collaboration with Sparky, Lee Mendelson, and Bill Melendez, which would be followed by five more specials. By 1999 he and Sparky had become close friends, and Benoit finished recording his latest project, *It's the Pied Piper, Charlie Brown,* just one day after Sparky's death.

Like many jazz artists, Benoit first heard Guaraldi's music on *A Charlie Brown Christmas.* "Guaraldi's playing was a pretty big influence on my own," said David Benoit, "and most of that influence came from watching the first animated television special when I was growing up. One of the reasons I got into playing jazz piano at all was because I liked the music from *A Charlie Brown Christmas* so much. That was the first time that jazz piano trio had been used in animation, which helped make it a really groundbreaking show. I agree with a lot of people who believe that a big part of the success of *A Charlie Brown Christmas* was Vince's music. In my mind, it made the whole show hip. It was just so different than all the cartoon sounds that had come before it. It always stuck with me, the way Guaraldi played jazz piano. It was

ABOVE RIGHT: Jazz pianist/composer David Benoit, who scored six *Peanuts* specials, with Charles Schulz.

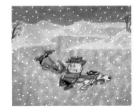

childlike and whimsical, always a bright feeling. He played from the heart and was a real communicator; he knew how to sit down at the piano and make people feel good.

"Guaraldi was one of the handful of pianists," reflected Benoit, "like Dave Brubeck and Andre Previn, who made jazz piano popular, who crossed that bridge. I think Vince may still be underrated as far as his place in jazz history, but he was a great jazz pianist."

Vince Guaraldi's legacy as a jazz innovator inspired the careers of contemporary jazz pianists and lives on as the "sound" of *Peanuts*. Those who knew Vince have not forgotten him, especially the creators of the *Peanuts* specials.

"He was a real good guy and we miss him," said Bill Melendez.

"The day of his funeral," recalled Lee Mendelson, "they played the Charlie Brown music over the sound system in the church. It was not an easy day; he was so young. It was one of the saddest days of my life. He was up to my house the night before and said he had not been feeling well, and didn't know what it was. It was totally unexpected.

"Vince Guaraldi's music is bright," said Lee. "I call it childlike. In the same way Bill kept the animation simple, Vince kept the music simple. This was jazz that appealed to both kids and adults, that captured the spirit of the characters. The music helped make the shows, and the shows helped make the music."

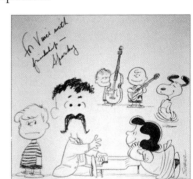

RIGHT: A personal greeting from Charles Schulz to Vince Guaraldi, complete with a cartoon caricature of the pianist sporting his signature handlebar mustache.

91

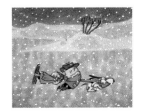

*the music of
vince guaraldi*

christmas time is here

music by vince guaraldi
lyrics by lee mendelson

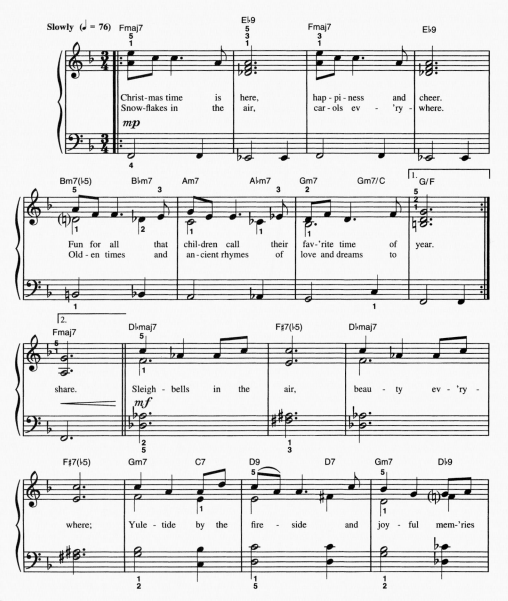

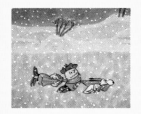

C7sus C7 Fmaj7 E♭9 Fmaj7
there. Christ - mas time is here, we'll be draw - ing
mp
E♭9 Bm7(♭5) B♭m7 Am7 A♭m7 Gm7 Gm7/C
near. Oh, that we could al - ways see such spir - it through the
Fmaj9 E♭9 Fmaj7 E♭9
year, through the year.
D♭maj7 F♯7(♭5) D♭maj7 F♯7(♭5)
mf
Gm7 C7 D9 D7 Gm7 D♭7 C7sus C7
Yule - tide by the fire - side and joy - ful mem-'ries there.
rit.

christmas time is here

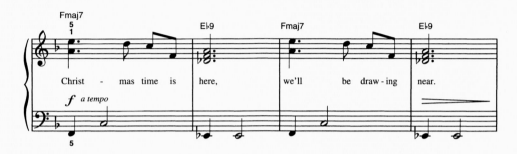

Christ - mas time is here, we'll be draw - ing near.

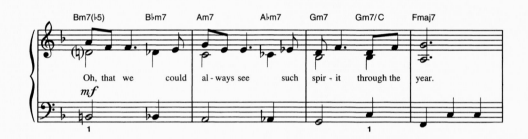

Oh, that we could al - ways see such spir - it through the year.

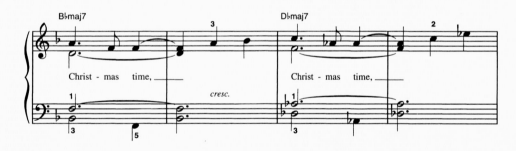

Christ - mas time, Christ - mas time,

cresc.

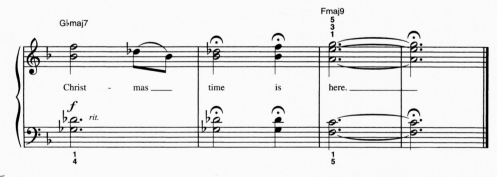

Christ - mas time is here.

f *rit.*

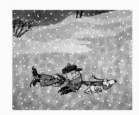

linus and lucy

by vince guaraldi

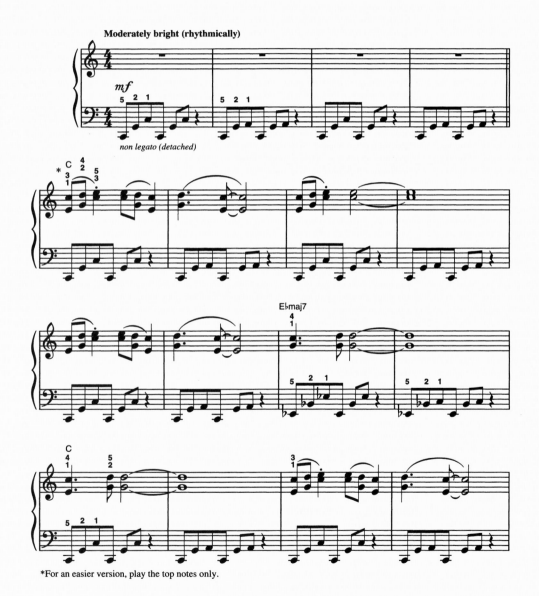

Moderately bright (rhythmically)

non legato (detached)

E♭maj7

*For an easier version, play the top notes only.

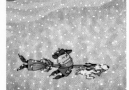

E♭
C
F
r.h.
F
C

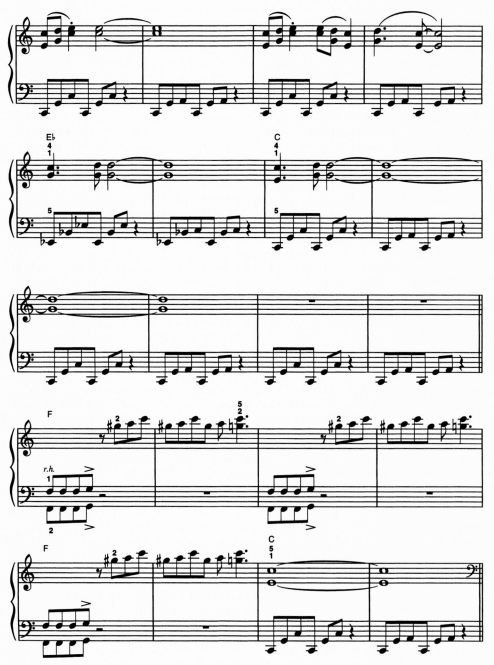

linus and lucy

E♭
C
E♭
C

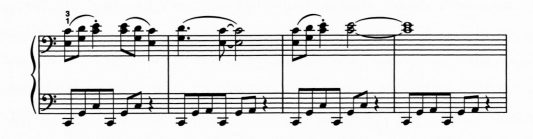

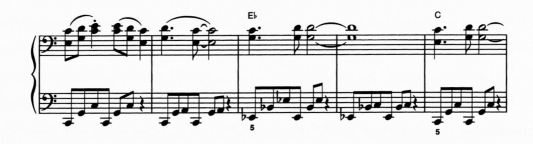

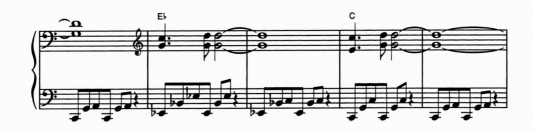

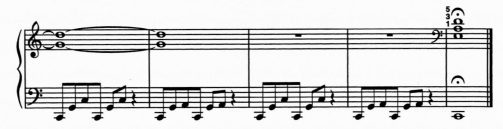

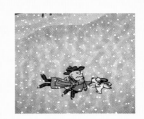

a charlie brown christmas

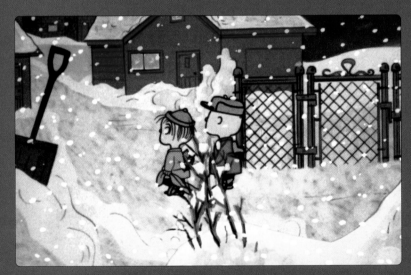
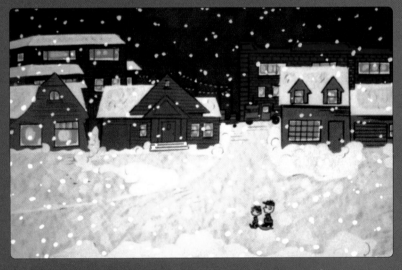

the illustrated script

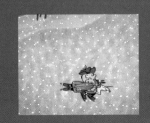

Pan winter scene; move to frozen pond where
children are skating and singing:

Christmas time is here,
Happiness and cheer,
Fun for all that children call
Their favorite time of year.
Snowflakes in the air,
Carols everywhere.
Olden times and ancient rhymes
Of love and dreams to share.

Fade in on Charlie Brown and Linus walking through
a light snowfall. They stop to talk over a brick wall

CHARLIE BROWN
I think there must be something wrong with
me, Linus. Christmas is coming, but I'm not
happy. I don't feel the way I'm supposed to feel.

They continue walking

CHARLIE BROWN *(cont.)*
I just don't understand Christmas, I guess. I might
be getting presents and sending Christmas cards
and decorating trees and all that, but I'm still not
happy. I always end up feeling depressed.

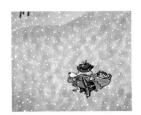

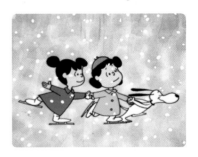

LINUS
Charlie Brown, you're the only person
I know who can take a wonderful
season like Christmas and turn it into
a problem. Maybe Lucy's right. Of all
the Charlie Browns in the world,
you're the Charlie Browniest.

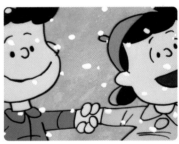

*They turn and walk toward skating pond.
The kids are skating and singing:*

Sleighbells in the air,
Beauty everywhere;
Yuletide by the fireside
And joyful memories there.
Christmas time is here,
Christmas time is here . . .

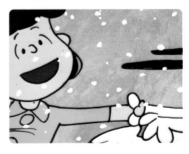

*Cut to Snoopy skating solo. He grabs
Lucy's hand and skates off. More kids
join hands to make a long tail. Snoopy
cracks the whip and kids fly in all directions*

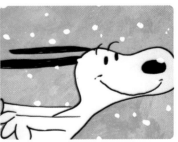

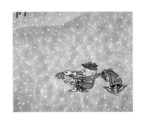

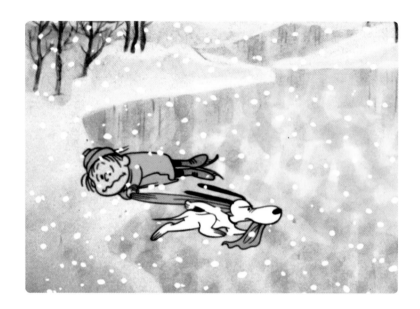 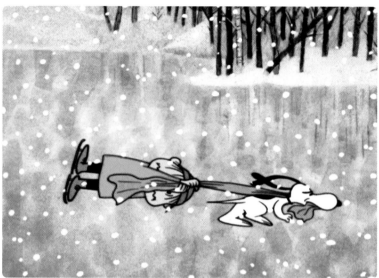

Snoopy is left spinning and comes to a stop as
Linus and Charlie Brown skate into the scene.
Snoopy charges in, grabs Linus's blanket in his
mouth and drags Linus off. As they race past
Charlie Brown, he gets caught in the blanket
and Snoopy spins them both around

Charlie Brown is snapped off, spins on the
ice and slides into a tree. A snow avalanche
falls over him and title appears over the shot:
A CHARLIE BROWN CHRISTMAS

A
CHARLIE
BROWN
Christmas

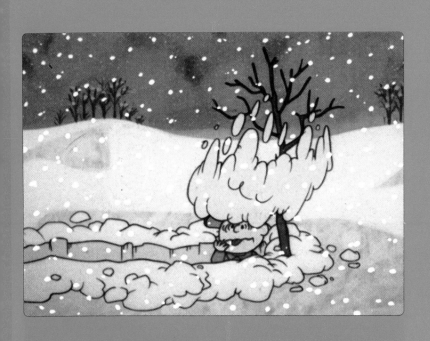

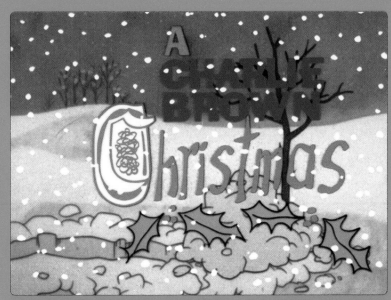

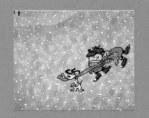

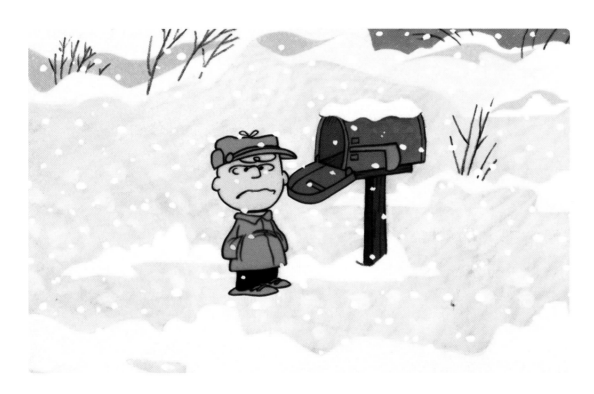

Cut to Charlie Brown at home, standing at the window watching the snow fall. He puts his coat on and goes outside to check the mailbox. He opens it and looks in:

CHARLIE BROWN
Hello in there!

Stands angrily next to the empty mailbox

CHARLIE BROWN
Rats! Nobody sent me a Christmas card today.

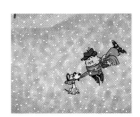

Begins walking

CHARLIE BROWN
I almost wish there weren't a holiday
season. I know nobody likes me.
Why do we have to have a holiday
season to emphasize it?

Meets up with Violet and Pig Pen

CHARLIE BROWN *(cont.)*
Thanks for the Christmas card you
sent me, Violet.

VIOLET
I didn't send you a Christmas card,
Charlie Brown.

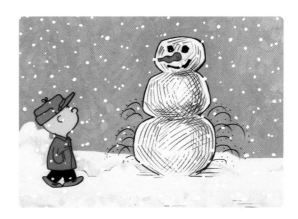

CHARLIE BROWN
Don't you know a sarcasm when
you hear it?

*Charlie Brown walks away and comes to a
large snowman. Pig Pen appears from behind
the snowman, patting the snow into place*

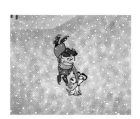

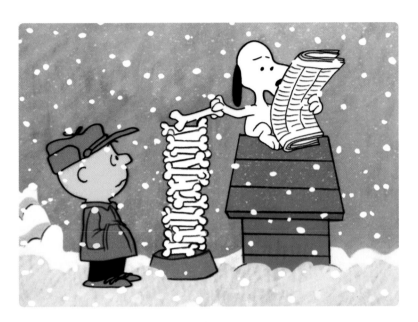

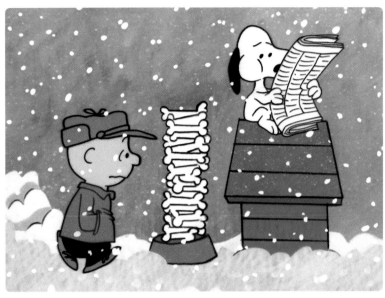

CHARLIE BROWN
Pig Pen, you're the only person I
know who can raise a cloud of dust
in a snowstorm.

*Charlie Brown walks along and stops at
Snoopy's doghouse. A tall pile of bones
rises from the dog dish. Snoopy reads a
newspaper and occasionally takes a bones
from the stack and munches it*

115

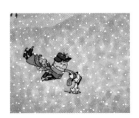

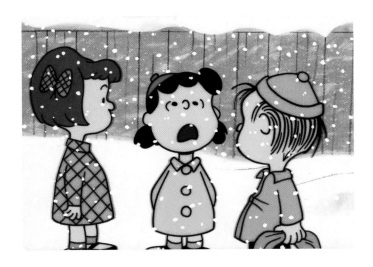

Charlie Brown continues walking and meets Schroeder, Patty, Lucy and Linus standing in the light snowfall

PATTY
Try to get snowflakes on your tongue. It's fun.

LUCY
Mm. Needs sugar. It's too early. I never eat December snowflakes. I always wait until January.

LINUS
They sure look ripe to me.

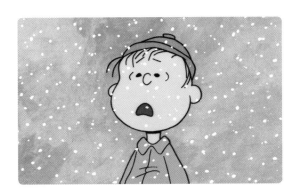

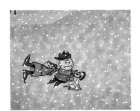

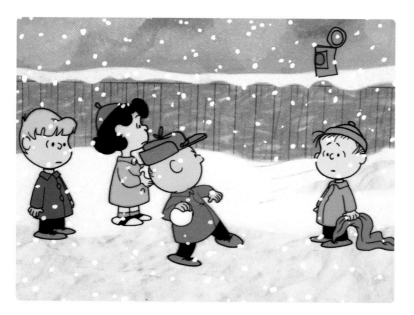 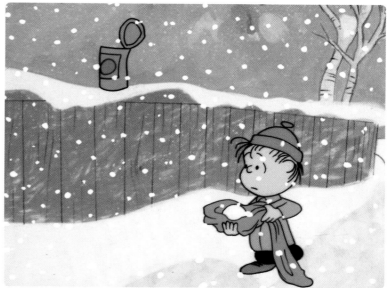

The kids try to knock a can off the wall with snowballs, with no success. Linus puts a snowball in his blanket and snaps it like a sling toward the can. He knocks the can off the wall and proudly walks past the group

LUCY *(to Linus)*
You think you're so smart with that blanket. What are you going to do with it when you grow up?

LINUS
Maybe I'll make it into a sport coat.

PSYCHIATRIC
HELP 5¢
THE
DOCTOR
IS
OUT

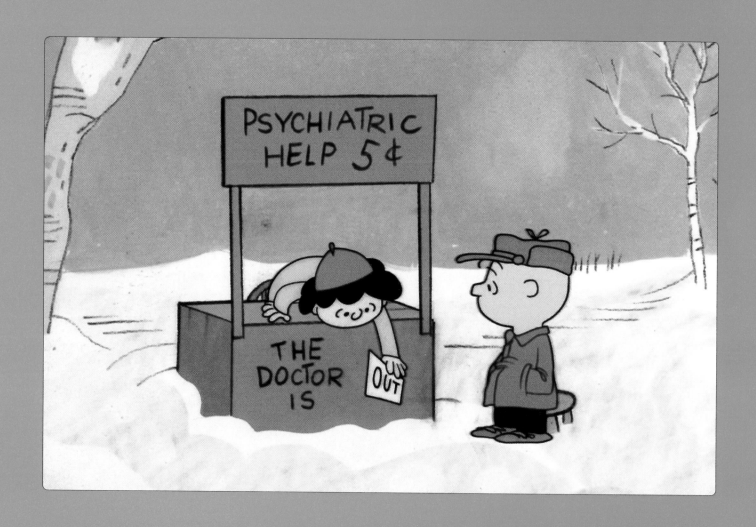

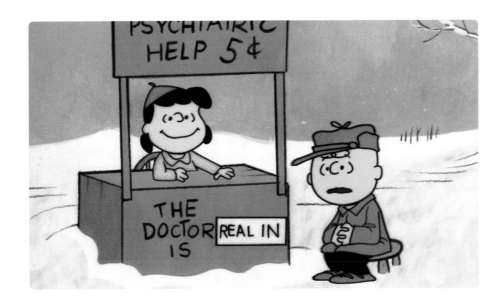

Charlie Brown walks over to Lucy's
psychiatric booth

Cut to Schroeder and Lucy

SCHROEDER *(to Lucy)*
I think you have a customer.

Lucy dashes over to the booth

LUCY
May I help you?

CHARLIE BROWN
I am in sad shape.

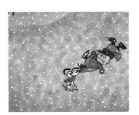

HELP 5¢
THE DOCTOR IS
REAL IN

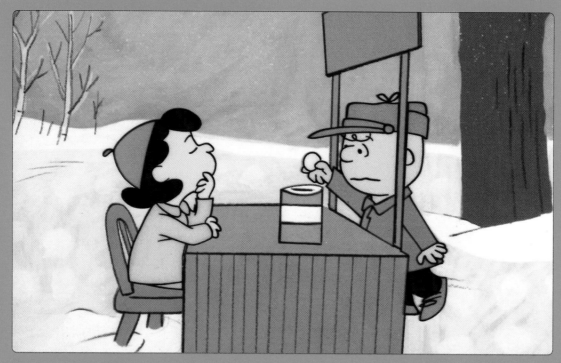

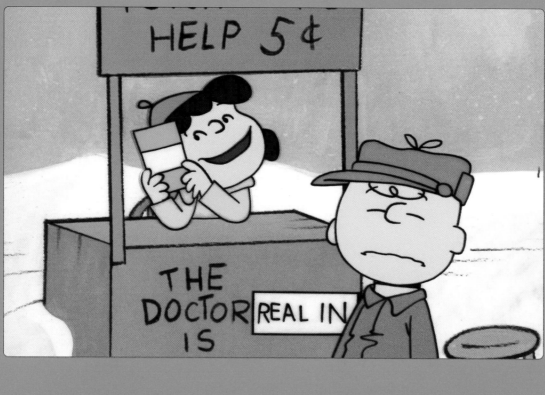

*Lucy hands Charlie Brown a can with a
money slot on top*

LUCY
Wait a minute. Before you begin, I
must ask that you pay in advance.
Five cents, please.

*Charlie Brown digs a nickel out of his pocket
and drops it in the can with a "clink"*

LUCY
Boy, what a sound. How I love hearing
that old money plate, that beautiful sound
of cold, hard cash. That beautiful, beautiful
sound. Nickels, nickels, nickels. That
beautiful sound of plunking nickels. All
right, now, what seems to be your trouble?

CHARLIE BROWN
I feel depressed. I know I should be
happy, but I'm not.

LUCY
Well, as they say on TV, the mere fact that
you realize you need help indicates that
you are not too far gone. I think we'd better

123

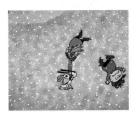

pinpoint your fears. If we can find out
what you're afraid of, we can label it. Are
you afraid of responsibility? If you are,
then you have hypengyophobia.

CHARLIE BROWN
I don't think that's quite it.

LUCY
How about cats? If you're afraid of cats,
you have ailurophasia.

CHARLIE BROWN
Well, sort of, but I'm not sure.

LUCY
Are you afraid of staircases? If you are,
then you have climacaphobia. Maybe
you have thalassophobia. This is fear of
the ocean, or gephyrobia, which is the
fear of crossing bridges. Or maybe you
have pantophobia. Do you think you
have pantophobia?

CHARLIE BROWN
What's pantophobia?

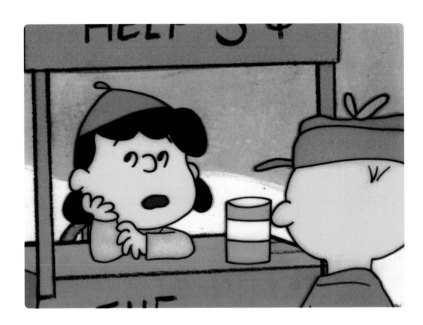

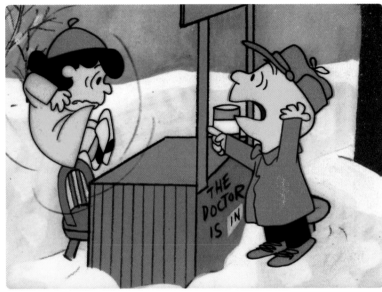

LUCY
The fear of everything.

CHARLIE BROWN
(Shouts) That's it!

Lucy is blown off her chair onto the ground

CHARLIE BROWN
Actually, Lucy, my trouble is Christmas.
I just don't understand it. Instead of
feeling happy, I feel sort of let down.

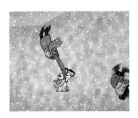

PSYCHIATRIC
HELP 5¢
THE
DOCTOR
IS
REAL IN

THE

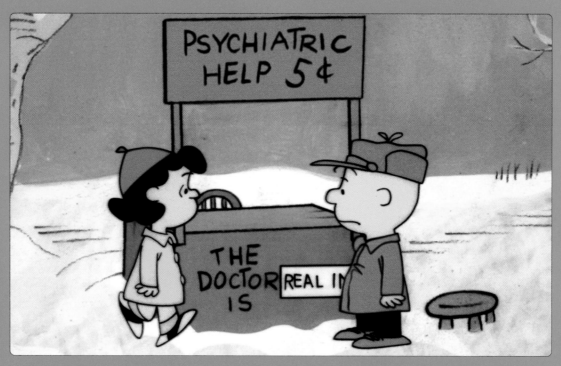

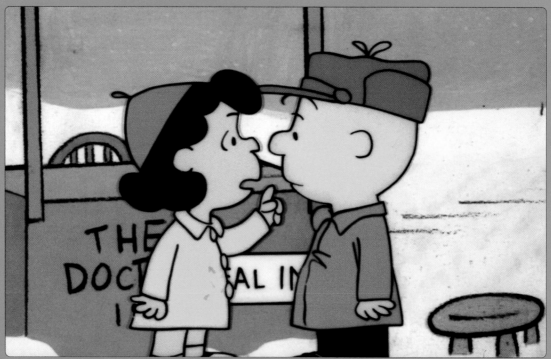

LUCY

You need involvement. You need to get involved in some real Christmas project. How would you like to be the director of our Christmas play?

CHARLIE BROWN

Me? You want me to be the director of the Christmas play?

LUCY

Sure, Charlie Brown. We need a director. You need involvement. We've got a shepherd, musicians, animals, everyone we need. We've even got a Christmas Queen.

CHARLIE BROWN

I don't know anything about directing a Christmas play.

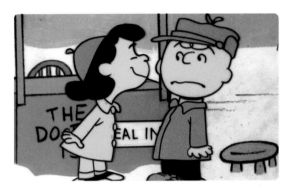

LUCY

Don't worry. I'll be there to help you. I'll meet you at the auditorium. Incidentally, I know how you feel about all this Christmas business, getting depressed and all that. *(Charlie Brown watches Snoopy walk past)* It happens to

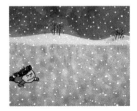

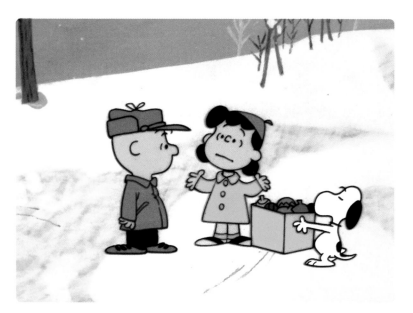

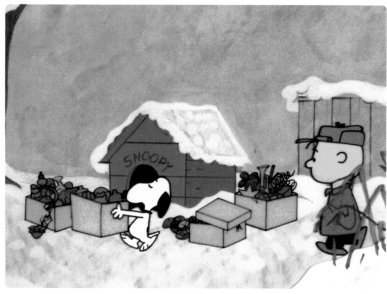

me every year. I never get what I really
want. I always get a lot of stupid toys or a
bicycle or clothes or something like that.

CHARLIE BROWN
What is it you want?

LUCY
Real estate.

*They both watch Snoopy walk past carrying a
box of Christmas lights and decorations. Charlie
Brown follows him. Snoopy begins building a
crazy display that covers his doghouse*

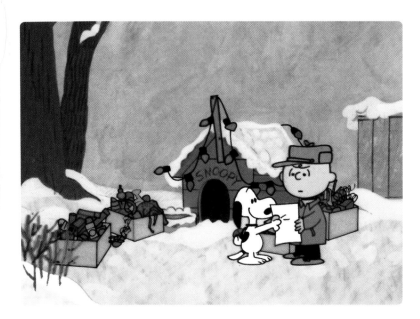

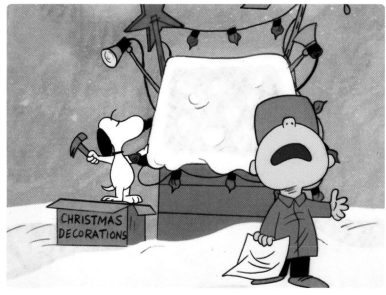

CHARLIE BROWN
What's going on here?

Snoopy hands him a piece of paper

CHARLIE BROWN *(cont.)*
What's this? *(Reading)* Find the true
meaning of Christmas. Win money,
money, money. Spectacular, supercolossal,
neighborhood Christmas lights and display
contest. *(Looks up from the paper)* Lights and
display contest! Oh, no. My own dog
gone commercial. I can't stand it!

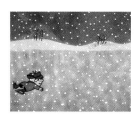

*Charlie Brown throws the paper in the air
and walks away. Meets Sally who is holding
a clipboard and pen*

SALLY
I've been looking for you, big brother.
Will you please write a letter to Santa
Claus for me?

CHARLIE BROWN
Well, I don't have much time. I'm
supposed to get down to the school
auditorium and direct the Christmas play.

SALLY
You write it and I'll tell you what I
want to say.

CHARLIE BROWN
Okay, shoot.

SALLY
Dear Santa Claus, how've you been?
How is your wife? Did you have a nice
summer? I wish it was. I have been
extra good this year, so I have a long
list of presents that I want.

131

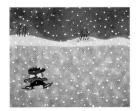

CHARLIE BROWN
Oh, brother.

SALLY
Please note the size and color of each item and send as many as possible. If it seems too complicated, make it easy on yourself. Just send money. How about tens and twenties?

CHARLIE BROWN
Tens and twenties? Oh, even my baby sister!

CHILD
All I want is what I have coming to me. All I want is my fair share.

Fade out. Open to new scene at the auditorium. Kids are all over the stage dancing to jazz music

Cut to Lucy

LUCY
All right, quiet, everybody. Our director will be here any minute and we'll start rehearsal.

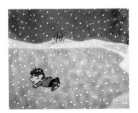

DIRECTOR

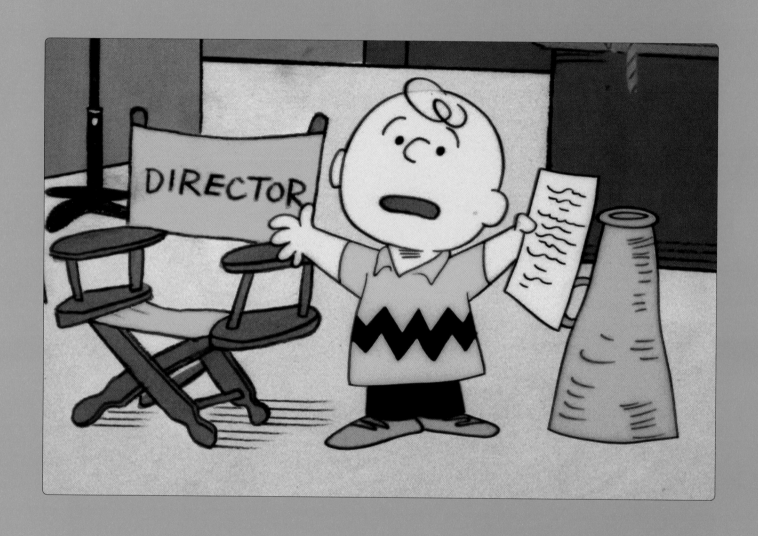

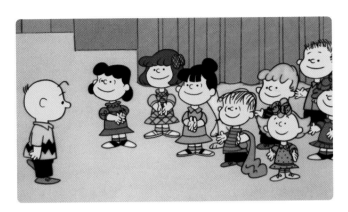
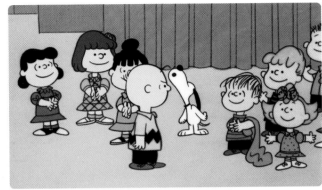

PATTY
Director? What director?

LUCY
Charlie Brown.

VIOLET
Oh, no! We're doomed!

PATTY
This will be the worst Christmas play ever.

LUCY
Here he comes! Attention, everyone!
Here's our director.

*General applause from the group except for one
"boo," which turns out to be from Snoopy.
Charlie Brown looks at him:*

CHARLIE BROWN
Man's best friend.

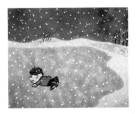

Charlie Brown walks over to the director's chair and addresses the kids

CHARLIE BROWN
Well, it's real good seeing you all here.
As you know, we are going to put on
the Christmas play. Due to the shortage
of time, we'll get right down to work.
One of the first things to ensure a good
performance, pay strict attention to the
director. I'll keep my direction simple.
If I point to the right, it means focus
attention stage right. If I make a slashing
motion across my throat, it means cut
the scene short. If I make a revolving
motion with my hand, it means pick up
the tempo. If I spread my hands apart,
it means slow down. It's the spirit of
the actors that counts. The interest that
they show in their director. Am I right?
I said, am I right?

*Cut to kids wildly dancing to "Linus
and Lucy" music. Charlie Brown picks
up megaphone*

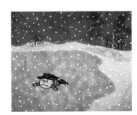

CHARLIE BROWN
Stop the music! All right, now. We're
going to do this play and we're going to
do it right. Lucy, get those costumes and
scripts and pass 'em out. Now, the script
girl will be handing out your parts.

*Lucy walks over to Frieda and hands her
a script and a costume*

LUCY
You're the innkeeper's wife.

FRIEDA *(bouncing her curls in her hand)*
Did innkeepers' wives have naturally
curly hair?

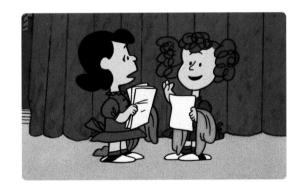

*Lucy walks over to Pig Pen and hands
him a script and a costume*

LUCY
Pig Pen, you're the innkeeper.

PIG PEN
In spite of my outward appearance,
I shall try to run a neat inn.

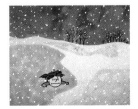

*Lucy walks over to Shermy and hands
him a script and a costume*

LUCY
Shermy, you're a shepherd.

SHERMY
Every Christmas it's the same. I always
end up playing a shepherd.

Lucy walks over to Snoopy and hands him a script

LUCY
Snoopy, you'll have to be all the animals
in our play. Can you be a sheep?

SNOOPY
Baaaaaa!

LUCY
How about a cow?

SNOOPY
Moooo!

LUCY
How about a penguin?

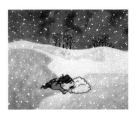

Snoopy walks around with his arms stiffly at his side, making clicking sounds with his feet

LUCY
Yes, he's even a good penguin.

Snoopy mugs around, acting out different animals, and sits on top of Lucy's head

LUCY
No, no, no!

Snoopy falls off her head

LUCY
Listen, all of you.

Snoopy stands behind Lucy and imitates her as she speaks to the group

LUCY
You've got to take direction. You've got to have discipline! You've got to have respect for your director!

Lucy turns around and catches Snoopy making fun of her

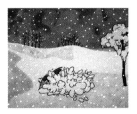

LUCY
I ought to slug you!

Snoopy kisses her

LUCY
Ugh! I've been kissed by a dog! I have
dog germs! Get hot water! Get some
disinfectant! Get some iodine!

Cut to Snoopy

SNOOPY
Aagh!

Cut to Charlie Brown with megaphone

CHARLIE BROWN
All right, all right, script girl. Continue
with the scripts.

Lucy walks over to Linus

LUCY
Linus, you've got to get rid of that stupid
blanket.

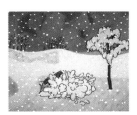

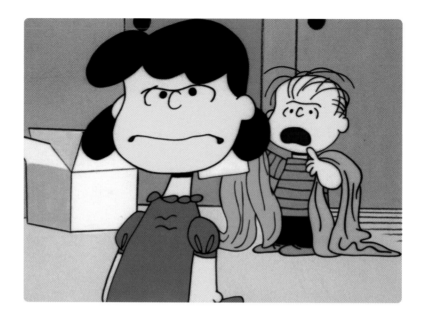

She hands him a script and costume

LUCY
And here, memorize these lines.

LINUS
I can't memorize these lines. This is
ridiculous.

LUCY
Memorize it and be ready to recite when
your cue comes.

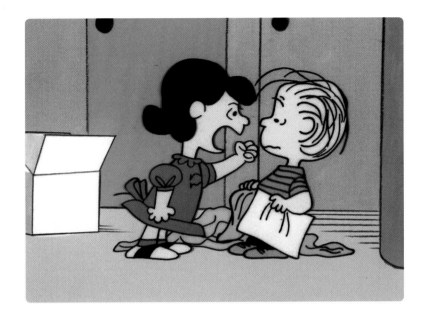

LINUS

I can't memorize something like this so quickly. Why should I be put through such agony? Give me one good reason why I should memorize this . . .

LUCY

I'll give you five good reasons.
(She makes a fist, one finger at a time)
One, two, three, four, five.

LINUS

Those are good reasons. Christmas is not only getting too commercial, it's getting too dangerous.

147

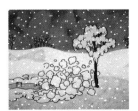

LUCY
And get rid of that stupid blanket! What's
a Christmas shepherd going to look like
holding a stupid blanket like that?

LINUS
Well, this is one Christmas shepherd
who's going to keep his trusty blanket
with him.

Linus quickly drapes his blanket over his head

LINUS
See? You wouldn't hit an innocent
shepherd, would you?

*Cut to Charlie Brown, trying to hold back
his temper. Lucy approaches him*

LUCY
Okay, Mr. Director. The cast is set.
Take over.

CHARLIE BROWN
All right. Let's have it quiet. Places,
everybody. Schroeder, set the mood
for the first scene.

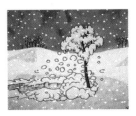

DIRECTOR

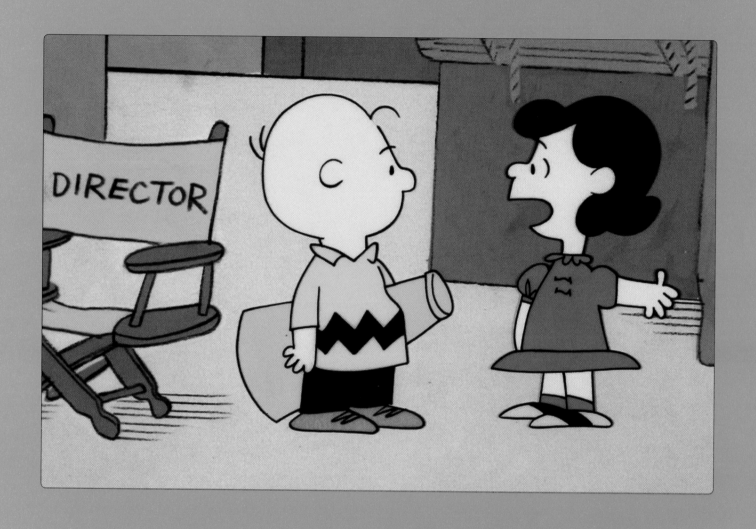

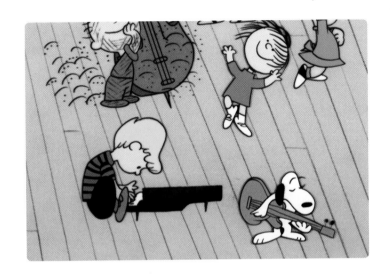

Schroeder begins playing "Linus and Lucy"
which sets the kids off dancing again

CHARLIE BROWN
Cut! Cut! No, no, no!

Walks over to Frieda and Pig Pen

CHARLIE BROWN
Look. Let's rehearse the scene at the inn.
Frieda . . .

FRIEDA
This can't go on. There's too much dust.
It's taking the curl out of my naturally
curly hair.

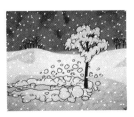

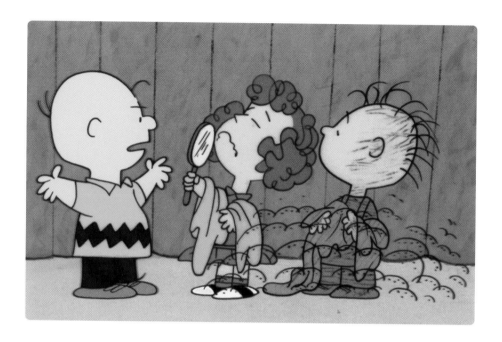

CHARLIE BROWN
Don't think of it as dust. Think of it
as maybe the soil of some great, past
civilization. Maybe the soil of ancient
Babylon. It staggers the imagination. You
may be carrying soil that was trod upon
by Solomon. Or even Nebuchadnezzar.

PIG PEN
Sort of makes you want to treat me with
more respect, doesn't it?

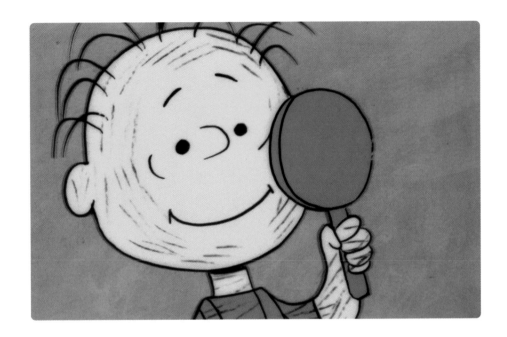

FRIEDA
You're an absolute mess. Just look
at yourself.

PIG PEN
On the contrary, I didn't think
I looked *that* good.

Cut to Charlie Brown and Linus

CHARLIE BROWN
Sally, come here.

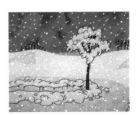

LINUS
What do you want her for?

CHARLIE BROWN
She's going to be your wife.

LINUS
Good grief.

Cut to Sally, clapping her hands gleefully, surrounded by hearts. She walks over to Linus and leans her head on his shoulder

SALLY
Isn't he the cutest thing? He has the nicest sense of humor.

LUCY
Lunch break. Lunch break.

CHARLIE BROWN
Lunch break?

Snoopy enters with his dish, kicking it and playing with it

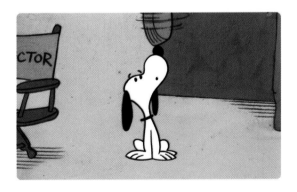

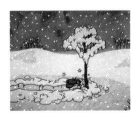

CHARLIE BROWN
All right, now. There's no time
for foolishness. We've got to get
on with our play.

LUCY
That's right. What about my part?
What about the Christmas Queen?
Hmm? Are you going to let all this
beauty go to waste? You do think I'm
beautiful, don't you, Charlie Brown?
You didn't answer me right away. You
had to think about it first, didn't you?
If you really had thought I was beautiful,
you would have spoken right up. I
know when I've been insulted. I
know when I've been insulted!

Exit Lucy

CHARLIE BROWN
Good grief. All right, let's take it
from the top again. Places. Action.

Kids dance to "Linus and Lucy"

Cut to Lucy and Charlie Brown

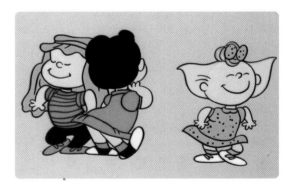

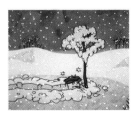

LUCY
Charlie Brown, isn't it a great play?

CHARLIE BROWN
That does it. Now, look. If we're ever
to get this play off the ground, you've
got to have some cooperation.

LUCY
What's the matter, Charlie Brown?
Don't you think it's great?

CHARLIE BROWN
It's all wrong.

LUCY
Look, Charlie. Let's face it. We all
know that Christmas is a big commercial
racket. It's run by a big eastern syndicate,
you know.

CHARLIE BROWN
Well, this is one play that's not going
to be commercial.

LUCY
Look, Charlie Brown. What do you want?

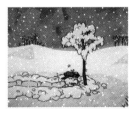

CHARLIE BROWN
The proper mood. We need
a Christmas tree.

LUCY
Hey, perhaps a tree. A great, big, shiny
aluminum Christmas tree. That's it,
Charlie Brown. You get the tree. I'll
handle this crowd.

The group gathers around them

CHARLIE BROWN
Okay. I'll take Linus with me. The rest
of you, practice your lines.

LUCY
Get the biggest aluminum tree you can
find, Charlie Brown. Maybe paint it pink.

PATTY
Yeah. Do something right for a change,
Charlie Brown.

Cut to Charlie Brown and Linus walking outside

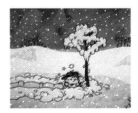

CHARLIE BROWN
I don't know, Linus. I just don't know.
Well, I guess we'd better concentrate on
finding a nice Christmas tree.

LINUS
I suggest we try those searchlights, Charlie
Brown.

*They enter a Christmas tree lot and Linus
knocks on an aluminum tree, making a
metallic clinking sound*

LINUS
This really brings Christmas close
to a person.

CHARLIE BROWN
Fantastic.

*Pan shot of various colorful trees. Zoom to
tiny pine tree on a wooden stand*

LINUS
Gee, do they still make wooden
Christmas trees?

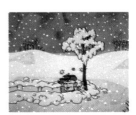

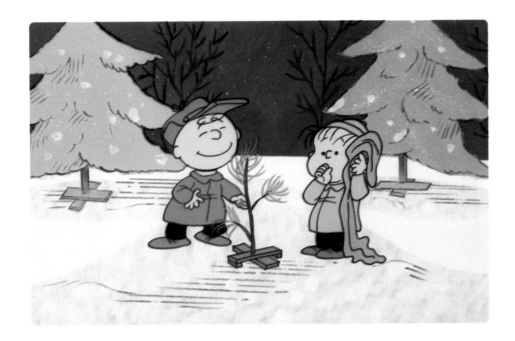

CHARLIE BROWN
This little green one here seems to need
a home.

LINUS
I don't know, Charlie Brown. Remember
what Lucy said? This doesn't seem to fit
the modern spirit.

CHARLIE BROWN
I don't care. We'll decorate it and it will
be just right for our play. Besides, I think
it needs me.

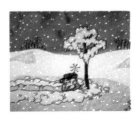

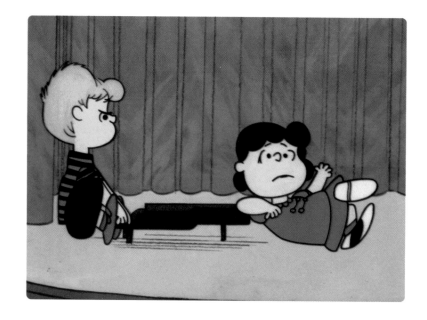

*Cut to Schroeder at the piano with Lucy leaning
on it at the far end*

SCHROEDER
This is the music I've selected for the
Christmas play.

Plays Beethoven's "Für Elise"

LUCY
What kind of Christmas music is that?

SCHROEDER
Beethoven Christmas music.

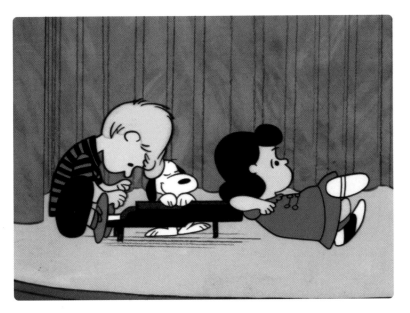

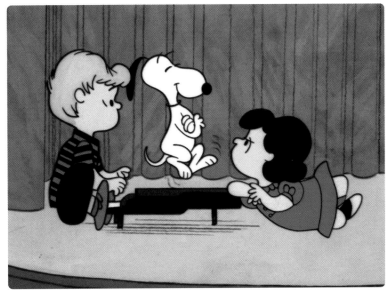

LUCY
What has Beethoven got to do with
Christmas? Everyone talks about how
great Beethoven was. Beethoven wasn't
so great.

SCHROEDER
(Angry) What do you mean Beethoven
wasn't so great?

LUCY
He never got his picture on bubble
gum cards, did he? Have you ever seen
his picture on a bubble gum card? Hmm?

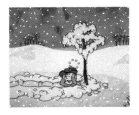

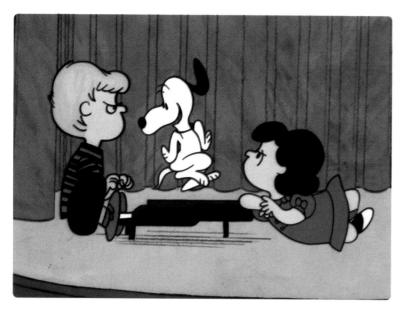

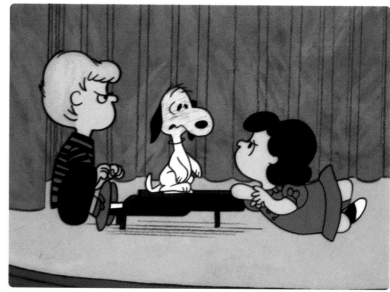

How can you say someone is great
who's never had his picture on bubble
gum cards?

SCHROEDER
Good grief.

*Begins to play jazz. Enter Snoopy, who
dances around and on top of the piano. He
keeps dancing after Schroeder has stopped
playing. Once he realizes the music has
stopped and that Schroeder and Lucy are
glaring at him, he blushes and slinks off.
Schroeder begins playing "Für Elise"*

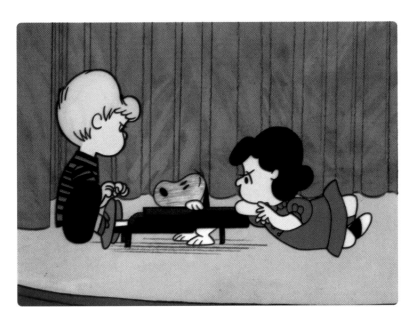

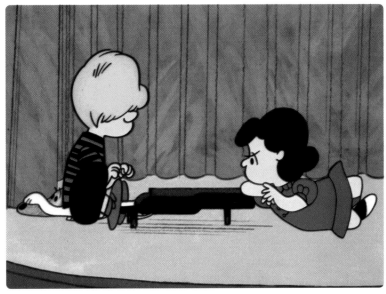

LUCY
Say, by the way, can you play "Jingle Bells"?

Schroeder plays "Jingle Bells" in classical style

LUCY
No, no. I mean "Jingle Bells." You know,
deck them halls and all that stuff.

He plays again with an organ sound

LUCY
No, no. You don't get it at all. I mean
"Jingle Bells." You know, Santa Claus and

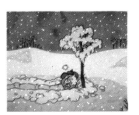

ho, ho, ho and mistletoe and presents
to pretty girls.

He taps out the melody with one finger

LUCY
(Shouts) That's it!

Schroeder is blown off his seat

*Cut to auditorium. Charlie Brown sets
the tree on top of Schroeder's piano.*

CHARLIE BROWN
We're back.

The kids gather around, astounded at the sad little tree

VIOLET
Boy, are you stupid, Charlie Brown.

PATTY
What kind of a tree is that?

LUCY
You were supposed to get a good tree. Can't you even tell a good tree from a poor tree?

VIOLET
I told you he'd goof it up. He's not the kind you can depend on to do anything right.

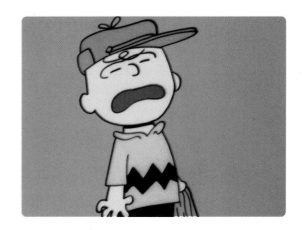

PATTY
You're hopeless, Charlie Brown.

FRIEDA
Completely hopeless.

CHARLIE BROWN
Rats.

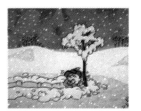

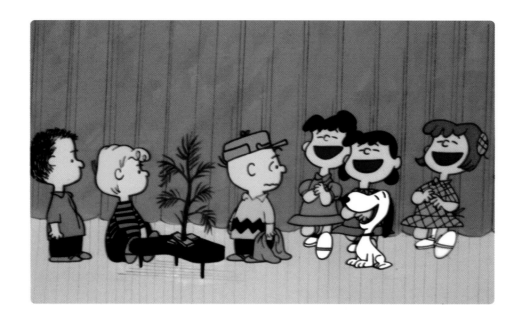

LUCY
You've been dumb before, Charlie Brown.
But this time, you really did it.

Kids and Snoopy laugh

LUCY
What a tree!

Kids walk away, except for Snoopy,
who continues to laugh, then exits.
Linus approaches Charlie Brown

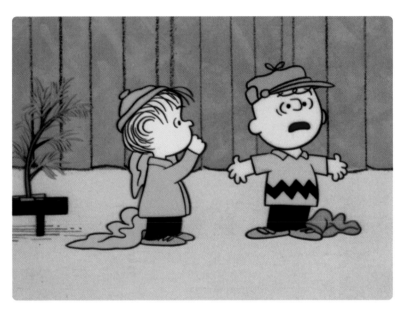

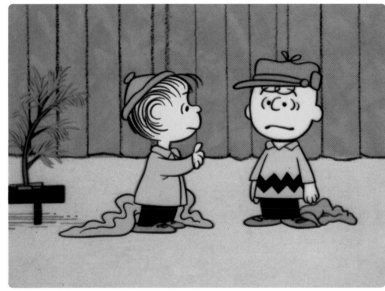

CHARLIE BROWN
I guess you were right, Linus. I shouldn't
have picked this little tree. Everything
I do turns into a disaster. I guess I really
don't know what Christmas is all about.
(Unhinged) Isn't there anyone who knows
what Christmas is all about?

LINUS
Sure, Charlie Brown. I can tell you
what Christmas is all about.

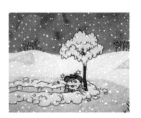

Linus walks to center stage, dragging his blanket

LINUS
Lights, please?

Auditorium lights dim and spot shines on Linus

LINUS
And there were in the same country shepherds abiding in the field, keeping watch over their flock by night. And lo, the angel of the Lord came upon them, and the glory of the Lord shown round about them. And they were sore afraid. And the angel said unto them, "Fear not, for behold, I bring you tidings of great joy which will be to all people. For unto you is born this day in the city of David a savior, which is Christ the Lord. And this shall be a sign unto you. Ye shall find the babe wrapped in swaddling clothes lying in a manger." And suddenly there was with the angel a multitude of the heavenly host, praising God and saying, "Glory to God in the highest, and on Earth peace, goodwill toward men."

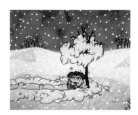

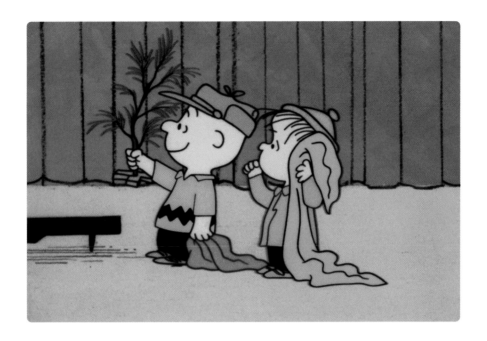

Picks up blanket and exits stage left.
Approaches Charlie Brown

LINUS
That's what Christmas is all about,
Charlie Brown.

Charlie Brown picks up the little tree and
walks out, past the group of quiet kids.
Enters the dark outdoors and gazes up at
the stars while remembering Linus's words

179

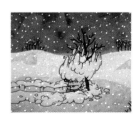

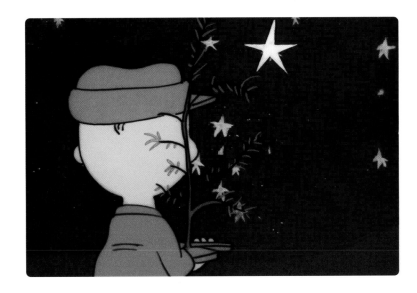

LINUS *(echo of previous speech)*
. . . for behold, I bring you tidings of
great joy which will be to all people.
For unto you is born this day in the city
of David a savior, which is Christ the
Lord. And this shall be a sign unto you.

CHARLIE BROWN
Linus is right. I won't let all this
commercialism ruin my Christmas.
I'll take this little tree home and
decorate it and I'll show them it
really will work in our play.

Fade out as Charlie walks into the distance

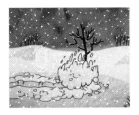

1ST

1ST

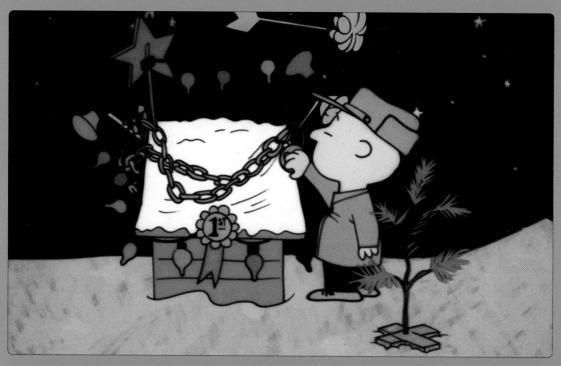

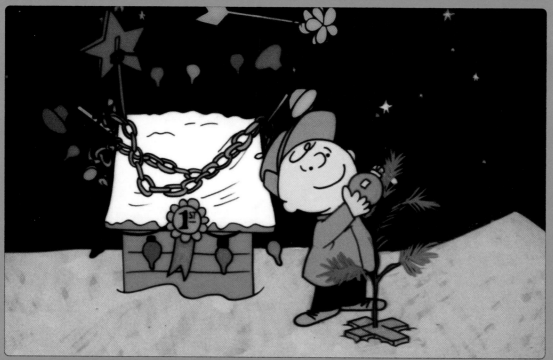

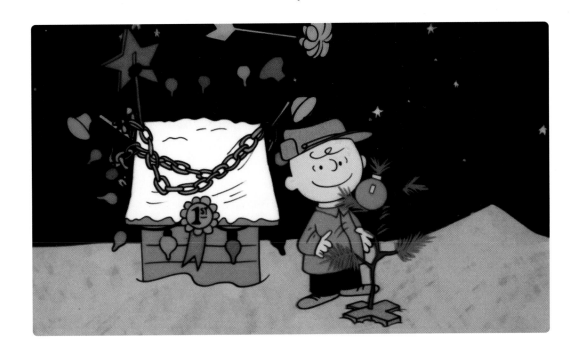

*Cut to Snoopy's crazily decorated doghouse.
Charlie Brown looks at the 1st prize ribbon*

CHARLIE BROWN
First prize? Oh, well, this commercial
dog is not going to ruin my Christmas.

*Charlie Brown happily sets the tree down.
Picks an ornament from the doghouse and
hangs it on the little tree. Tree slumps way
over from the weight of the bulb*

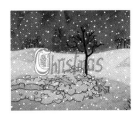

1ST

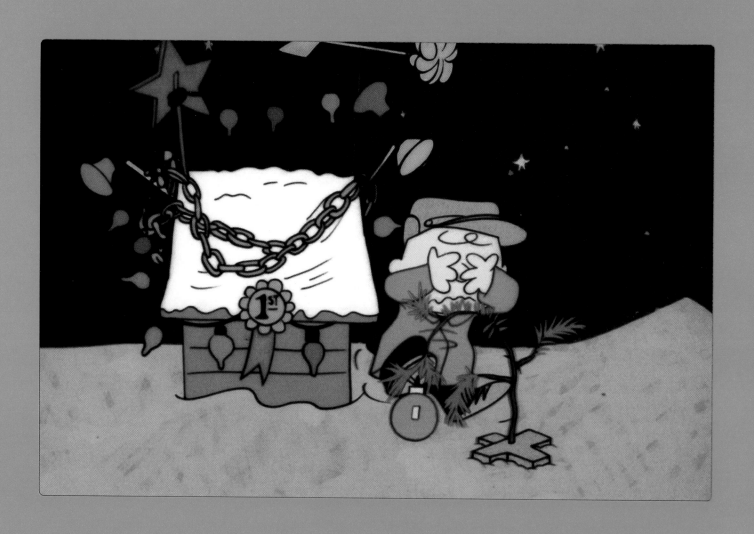

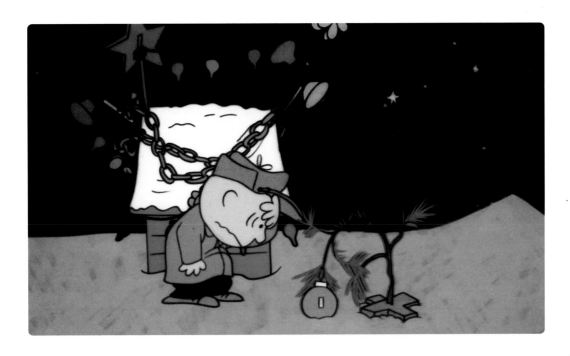

CHARLIE BROWN
I've killed it!
(Complete disgust and resignation)
Oh, everything I touch gets ruined!

*Charlie Brown exits, leaving the
sad little tree*

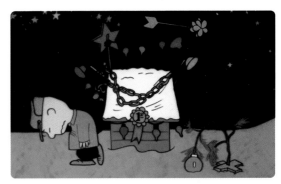

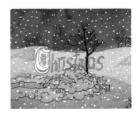

185

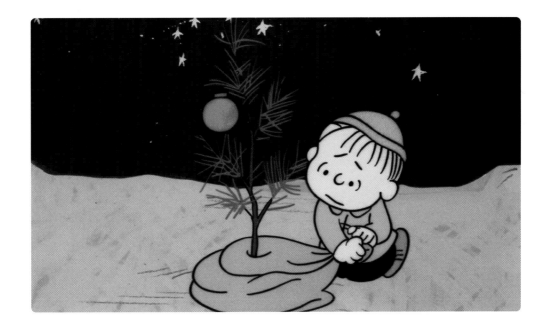

Kids enter and gather around tree

LINUS
I never thought it was such a bad little tree.

*Linus pulls up the droopy branch, straightens it
and wraps his blanket around the base of the tree*

LINUS
It's not bad at all, really. Maybe it just
needs a little love.

*Pan to kids, tree and decorated doghouse.
The kids takes ornaments from the doghouse
and decorate the tree, transforming it into a
lush, beautiful Christmas tree*

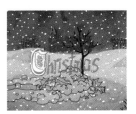

A
Christmas

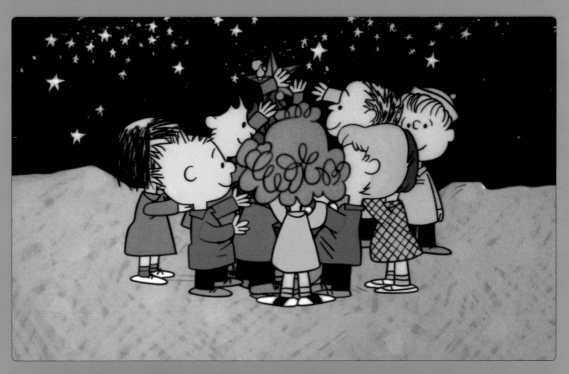

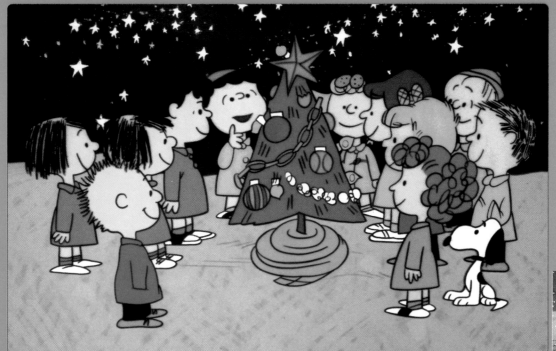

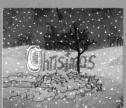

LUCY
Charlie Brown is a blockhead, but he did
get a nice tree.

Kids hum "O Little Town of Bethlehem"
Enter Charlie Brown

CHARLIE BROWN
What's going on here?

CHILDREN *(shout in unison)*
Merry Christmas, Charlie Brown!

Charlie Brown smiles and joins the festivities.
Kids sing "Hark the Herald Angels Sing"

Hark, the herald angels sing,
Glory to the newborn King!
Peace on Earth and mercy mild,
God and sinner reconciled.
Joyful, all ye nations, rise!
Join the triumph of the skies!
With angelic host proclaim:
Christ is born in Bethlehem.
Hark, the herald angels sing,
Glory to the newborn King.

THE END

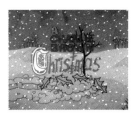

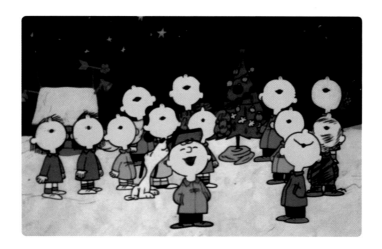

CREDITS

WRITTEN BY **Charles M. Schulz**
DIRECTED BY **Bill Melendez**
EXECUTIVE PRODUCER: **Lee Mendelson**
ORIGINAL SCORE COMPOSED
AND CONDUCTED BY **Vince Guaraldi**

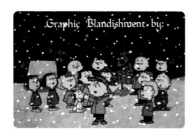

Ed Levitt
Bernard Gruver
Ruth Kissane
Dean Spille
Beverly Robbins

Eleanor Warren
Frank Smith
Bob Carlson
Rudy Zamora
Bill Littlejohn
Alan Zaslove
Ruben Timmins
Herman Cohen
Manuel Perez
Russ von Neida
John Walker

EDITING: **Robert T. Gillis**

SOUND: **Producers Sound Service**

A Lee Mendelson–Bill Melendez Production
in cooperation with United Feature Syndicate, Inc.